THE READING OF VIMALAKIRTI

First Printing, 2025

Published by dFRAE Media Co., Lexington, Kentucky

This work is a derivative of the *Vimalakirti Nirdesa Sutra,* an ancient
Buddhist sutra that is believed to have been written around 100 CE
in India. My translation and interpretation presented here honor
the core meaning and intent of the original texts while making them
accessible to modern queer practitioners. While I use contemporary
language and cultural references, I maintain deep respect for the
profound wisdom these ancient teachings contain.

THE READING OF VIMALAKIRTI

DAVID FRANKLIN SPARKS

Contents

Preface: The Divine Shade of Vimalakirti   vii

Homage   xi

  1 The Divine Display   1

  2 A Lesson in Spiritual Vision   5

  3 Strategy of Sickness   13

  4 Everyone Had Their Excuses Ready   23

  5 Reading Sickness For Filth   29

  6 Inconceivable Liberation   35

  7 The Goddess   47

  8 The Scenic Route   57

  9 Non-Duality   67

10 The Fragrant Feast   71

11 Unitl The Food's Digested   83

12 The Whole Truth Buffet   91

Analysis: Vimalakirti For A Modern World   97
About the Author   103

Preface: The Divine Shade of Vimalakirti

Back in the early centuries of Buddhism, someone wrote an absolutely legendary sutra featuring what might be the fiercest character in Buddhist literature. In the same way that Greek myths gave us archetypal figures like Prometheus and Odysseus, the Vimalakirti Sutra gave Buddhism its ultimate enlightened householder—a character who turned spiritual teaching into performance art and served dharma with a side of divine shade.

Picture the scene this ancient text paints for us: A mansion in the city of Vaishali where a crowd is gathering—monks, merchants, courtesans, princes—all drawn to a sickroom where our protagonist holds court. Like all great teaching stories, the tale of Vimalakirti uses theatrical elements and magical moments to deliver profound truths about transformation and awakening.

In this sacred drama, Vimalakirti wasn't your typical spiritual teacher. The story follows him moving through every realm of society—courts, markets, pleasure quarters, temples—wearing each role like a costume while teaching liberation. When monks preached about renouncing the world, he showed up in designer robes to teach about emptiness. When ascetics bragged about their strict practices, he hosted legendary feasts that turned into dharma teachings. And when anyone got too full of their own spiritual accomplishments, Vimalakirti was there with a reality check served with enough style to make RuPaul take notes.

But this wasn't just spiritual theater. Through Vimalakirti's character, the sutra embodies a profound truth about liberation—that everything, absolutely everything, can be transformed into the path of awakening. His legendary "illness" wasn't just some divine performance art. It was a teaching about how we all experience the fundamental sickness of cyclic existence, and more importantly, how we can transform that very suffering into the path to freedom.

For us practitioners today, especially those of us navigating queer lives and bodies in a world that often misunderstands both, the story of Vimalakirti is pure gold. Whether we take it as historical truth or meaningful myth, its lessons show us how to work with whatever arises—illness, desire, social roles, shade-throwing and all—as fuel for awakening. Let's dive into this legendary tale of dharma and drama, and learn how to transform every aspect of our messy, beautiful lives into opportunities for liberation.

WHO WAS THIS QUEEN OF DHARMA?

The Vimalakirti Sutra introduces us to its title character like that friend who somehow belongs everywhere and nowhere at once. Rich? Absolutely. He's living in a mansion that makes Architectural Digest look basic. Married? Yes, with kids and everything. Showing up at the palace to advise kings? Check. Rolling through the marketplace teaching merchants about profit and loss? That too. Drinking with courtesans while dropping truth bombs about desire? All of it.

But here's the thing—he's doing all this while being fully enlightened. The sutra tells us he's only playing these worldly roles as a form of "skillful means," using each situation to help different beings wake up. He's serving different looks not because he's trapped in delusion, but because he's skilled enough to work every realm for the benefit of others.

This is what made him such a revolutionary figure in Buddhist literature. Until this story came along, most Buddhist texts focused on monastics who'd renounced the world. But Vimalakirti showed up in lay clothes and basically said, "Honey, liberation isn't about what you're wearing—it's about how you're seeing."

And about that infamous illness? In the sutra, Vimalakirti takes to his sickbed in what has to be one of the most dramatic teaching moments in spiritual history. When people come to visit him—which is exactly what he planned—he turns his "illness" into a lesson about how we're all sick with the chronic condition of cyclic existence. Sariputra shows up trying to be all proper and proper, and Vimalakirti reads him for filth: "Girl, your real sickness is the concept of 'self' you're clutching like last season's robes."

But here's what makes this story so relevant for us today: Vimalakirti shows us that we don't have to choose between being engaged in the world and being on a spiritual path. We don't have to pick between serving face and serving dharma. The secret is transforming everything—our jobs, our relationships, our struggles, even our fabulousness—into opportunities for awakening.

—David Franklin Sparks
January 2025
Lexington, Kentucky

HOMAGE

*Bestowing the utmost respect
to the legendary icons:*

*The Buddhas,
The spiritual influencers,
The noble followers,
And independent practitioners
who found their own path.*

*Past, present, and future.
Serving enlightened realness:*

Period.

1

The Divine Display

So here's the tea: The gathering went down at Amrapali's mango grove. And trust, no one understood the assignment like she did. The same garden where princes left crownshaped indents in her silk cushions. Where her laugh started wars. Now the scent of sandalwood incense wrapped around the mango trees, mixing with the lingering perfume of her famous parties.

When I say the crowd was everything, I mean EVERYTHING.

The bodhisattvas came through first, thirty-two thousand deep. Their feet barely touched the ground, leaving lotus petals where their steps should've been. When they spoke, truth dripped like honey from their lips, echoing through the ten directions like a house mother's call. The moment any doubt tried to enter the chat, they shut it down with a single raised eyebrow.

Then the arhats rolled up, eight thousand beings who'd cracked the code of existence. They didn't walk so much as float, their robes rippling in winds no one else could feel. One caught a falling blossom before it touched the ground. Another whispered a word that turned storm clouds to clear sky. A third's smile stopped time in its tracks. Main character energy but make it humble.

Their breath moved in sync with the universe's pulse. When they spoke, every language on earth fell from their lips like they had divine Google Translate installed in their souls. The grass beneath their feet bloomed out of season. Birds changed their songs to match their footsteps.

The gods didn't just show up - they descended. Thousands of them piercing through the veils between worlds like light through crystal. Their wings folded into shoulder blades, their halos tucked away like hidden jewelry. Brahma Sikhin from the Asoka universe led them in, their very atoms rearranging to fit into earthly form, serving four-dimensional realness.

In the pavilion where Amrapali once made kings stammer, Buddha sat. The mango trees that had shaded a thousand secret rendezvous now bent their branches toward him like courtiers bowing. Light pooled at his feet, climbed up the walls, turned the air to liquid gold. The crowd swayed toward him like grass in the wind, angels and arhats alike tipping forward as if gravity itself had shifted its center.

The Licchavis swept in wearing silks dyed with gold dust, their fingers stacked with rings that could buy whole villages.

Even their servants' servants wore pearls. Young Ratnakara led the parade, five hundred nobles moving like a single organism, each carrying a parasol that caught light and turned it into rainbows. Seven types of precious gems in each one, throwing patterns on the ground like shattered kaleidoscopes.

Their circuit around Buddha was a choreographed fever dream. Seven circles, clockwise, feet moving in perfect sync. When they laid down their parasols, the sound of jewels touching earth rang like temple bells.

Buddha didn't speak. Didn't move. But power rolled off him in waves.

The parasols melted into each other. Merged. Stretched. What was solid became light became sky became everything. A canopy huge enough to cover a billion worlds, reflecting everything back at once.

Look up:

There's the snow just falling on the mountain

There's the first lotus opening in a pond

There's a baby taking their first steps in a country that hasn't been named yet

There's a star being born in a galaxy we'll never reach

The voices of all the Buddhas from every realm of existence rang through it, wisdom raining down like star showers. Each droplet of celestial surround sound carrying truth that could shake mountains.

The crowd held their breath. Even the gods, who'd danced on solar flares and played tag with comets, pressed their hands to their mouths. Celestial jaws? Dropped. Divine wigs? Snatched. The moment stretched like taffy, sweet and endless.

In Amrapali's garden, where desire had once been an art form, even wanting stopped to watch.

2

A Lesson in Spiritual Vision

The air in Amrapali's garden crackled like divine static as Ratnakara stepped forward. His silk robes caught the light from a thousand universes, each fold throwing rainbows that hadn't been invented yet. The young noble's fingers trembled—imagine standing in a garden party where the ceiling was literally the entire cosmos, surrounded by beings who glowed like walking supernovas, about to deliver a speech that would echo through millennia.

He dropped to one knee, his posture serving medieval fantasy realness so correct it made the actual gods in attendance take notes. When he opened his mouth, pure poetry dripped like honey from his lips:

"Those eyes though—" His voice caught the garden's light and threw it back amplified. "Pure as lotus petals floating on still water, but make it transcendent." His hands painted shapes in the air as he spoke, leaving trails of light that formed momentary mandalas. "That mind? Already been there, done that with every kind of meditation, collected all the spiritual badges, but somehow making it look effortless."

The mango trees leaned closer, their leaves shivering with anticipation. A fallen petal spiraled between them, existing in seven different colors.

"While we're out here drowning in our karma, looking like spiritual mess..." Ratnakara gestured at himself and his crew, their jewels catching starlight from galaxies that hadn't formed yet. "You're existing in perfect peace like it's no big thing. The ocean of your good qualities? Honey, we can't even see the horizon."

Buddha's smile could have lit up a thousand dark ages. His fingers traced patterns in the air that looked like casual gestures but were actually rearranging reality at a quantum level. The grass beneath him sprouted tiny flowers that bloomed in impossible colors.

When Ratnakara finished his divine read of praise, he flourished those silk sleeves one more time. "So listen—" His voice shifted from poetry to pure purpose. "These 500 young nobles with me? They're trying to achieve complete enlightenment, but make it fashion. They want to know how enlightened beings purify their realms. Break it down for us?"

The light around Buddha's shoulders stood up and paid attention. His eyes crinkled at the corners like someone who'd heard the exact question they'd been waiting centuries for someone to ask. The air around him began to sparkle, as if reality itself was about to spill some cosmic tea.

"Now that," he said, as his voice started throwing light, "is what I'm talking about."

The crowd leaned in so hard they nearly tipped over their lotus thrones. Even the gods were conjuring divine notepads, their pens hovering over pages made of condensed starlight. A peacock strutted past, its tail feathers displaying scenes from all possible universes.

Buddha picked up a fallen mango leaf, turning it over in hands that had mapped the geography of enlightenment. "Everyone thinks enlightened realms are these far-off places," he said, watching light play across the leaf's surface. "Like some cosmic gated community with a really strict HOA."

Robes rustled as several monks shifted uncomfortably, their brows furrowed like spiritual math wasn't mathing. Buddha caught a young one's fingers twisting in his lap, saw the questions gathering behind his eyes like storm clouds. The mango trees dipped their branches lower, as if they too wanted to catch every word.

Buddha swept his gaze across the gathered beings, his eyes meeting theirs in ways that rewrote their understanding of what eyes could do. "Your realm grows every time you choose generosity over greed. It gets stronger when you do the right thing, even while your ego is throwing a tantrum. It expands with every breath of patience, every push against what's easy."

The air in the garden was getting thicker with wisdom, hanging like sweet mist between the mango trees. Even the most enlightened beings were perched on the edges of their lotus seats, their halos tilting forward in anticipation.

That's when Sariputra's thoughts crashed the party.

Now, Sariputra was that disciple who'd read every book in the spiritual library but sometimes couldn't see the enlightenment for the trees. Buddha had arranged this whole moment - planting the doubt in Sariputra's mind like a seed that was about to flower into the most iconic teaching moment of the afternoon.

There he sat, his brows knitted together like they were trying to solve a cosmic puzzle. He was thinking loud enough for every psychic in three dimensions to hear: "Wait... if an enlightened being's realm reflects their mind, and Buddha is literally That Girl... why does this place look so... basic?"

Buddha's smile curved like a cat who'd watched a mouse walk straight into the trap. "Sariputra," he called out, his voice dripping honey and a touch of shade, "When people are born blind and can't see the sun and moon, is that the celestial bodies' fault?"

Sariputra, walking right into it like he had a map: "No, of course not. That limitation belongs to those born blind, not to the sun and moon."

"Exactly." Buddha's tone could have cut diamonds. "So if certain beings can't see the magnificence of my realm, maybe that says more about their spiritual cataracts than my interior design choices?"

The crowd went absolutely still. Even the mango trees held their breath.

But Brahma Sikhin, that cosmic defender that he was, rose from his throne of condensed starlight. "Sariputra, darling, let me stop you right there. I'm seeing Buddha's realm right now, and it's serving the same energy as the highest divine palaces."

Sariputra, apparently determined to dig himself deeper: "Well, from where I'm sitting, I see this earth with all its bumps and messiness. Like, literally, there's trash."

Brahma Sikhin's eyebrow arched so high it nearly achieved its own enlightenment. "The fact that you see it that way just proves your mind is giving very much spiritual astigmatism. Those of us who've done our inner work? We're seeing paradise, hun."

That's when Buddha decided to end the debate with a move so iconic it would be referenced for millennia. He simply touched one toe to the ground - the smallest gesture carrying the biggest "watch this" energy.

The transformation rolled out like a wave of pure fabulousness. The entire billion-world galaxy crystallized into an array of precious jewels that had gemologists in every realm questioning their career choices. Every being present found themselves seated on thrones that made their previous divine furniture look like plastic lawn chairs. The whole realm sparkled like it had been designed by someone who looked at the cosmos and said "Yes, but what if it sparkled more?"

Buddha turned to Sariputra, who was now perched on his own crystal throne looking like he wished he'd kept his observations in drafts. "How's the view now, Beloved?"

Sariputra managed to whisper, "I... I've never seen anything like this." His voice trembled like he'd just realized he'd been wearing spiritual sunglasses indoors this whole time.

Buddha settled deeper into his throne, each movement casting prisms of light that wrote sutras in the air. "Here's the tea about my realm - it's always this pure. I keep it looking basic most of the time to help y'all with less spiritual development level up. Think of it like this: the gods of the Thirty-Three Realms all eat from the same divine vessel, but what they taste depends on their own spiritual credit score. Same principle. Everyone's looking at the same realm, but what they see? That's between them and their spiritual optometrist."

The impact rippled through the crowd like the world's most enlightened wave. Eighty-four thousand beings got it, their faces lighting up like smartphones at a concert except the light was coming from inside. The five hundred young nobles who'd come with Ratnakara? Their understanding upgraded from spiritual dial-up to cosmic 5G in that single moment.

Then Buddha, having made his point with all the subtlety of a divine disco ball, withdrew his power. The realm shifted back to its regular appearance - though now everyone was looking at it with eyes that had been permanently adjusted. Some of the more traditional disciples started mumbling about impermanence, missing the point harder than a meteorite missing Earth.

The final tally was giving enlightenment realness: Thirty-two thousand beings developed perfect spiritual vision. Eight thousand monastics had their minds so liberated they could no longer find their delusions. And those eighty-four thousand beings who'd witnessed the whole display? They saw through the entire illusion of reality and said 'Sign me up for that enlightenment waiting list.'

Not bad for one afternoon in a courtesan's pleasure garden.

Through it all, Amrapali's mango trees kept swaying in the breeze, their leaves whispering ancient gossip about the times they'd seen - from hosting the messiest elite to witnessing the most iconic spiritual flex. Talk about a glow-up for the ages.

3

Strategy of Sickness

The light in Vaishali was different that spring. It caught the edges of things—silk robes, carved doorways, beggars' bowls—and turned them momentarily infinite, like everyday objects remembering they were made of star stuff. In the marketplace, mangoes gleamed with impossible colors while vendors argued about prices in three different realities at once. And through it all moved Vimalakirti, their presence making the air itself hold its breath.

They weren't what you'd expect from someone who'd cracked the code of existence. No dramatic robes, no floating lotus petals, clean lines and immaculate tailoring that somehow made couture look try-hard. The kind of simple elegance that spoke of old money, except the wealth they carried couldn't be inherited or stolen. Their moves were precise as calligraphy, each gesture writing liberation in languages that wouldn't be invented for centuries.

On paper, they had what the nobles called "the complete set"—the kind of mansion that would make architects weep, family straight out of a celestial sitcom, social connections that could make or break three different karmic cycles. But watch how they moved through it all. Like someone reading a story they'd memorized long ago, knowing every plot point but not quite believing in the characters anymore. Their body was a temple, but make it minimalist: swept clean, empty enough to echo, not a trace of ego-dust on any surface.

The marketplace knew them. Every vendor had a story about the time Vimalakirti showed up at their stall and casually rearranged their entire existence while haggling over mangoes. They moved through the morning crowd like water through silk, stopping here to help a farmer calculate her profits (and slides in a lesson about impermanence), there to settle a dispute between merchants (while demonstrating the empty nature of all possession). The fruit seller who tried to slip a few overripe mangoes into their basket? Got such a gentle lesson in ethics that she ended up crying behind her stall, not from shame but from suddenly understanding something she'd been missing her whole life.

In the palace, they were giving enlightened chameleon energy. One minute breaking down the emptiness of political power to ministers who thought they were making small talk about the weather, next minute in the royal gardens showing nobles how their designer dharma was last season's attachment in a fancy package. They'd roll into high-level political meetings and read everyone's power plays like they were large-print picture books, then flip the script so smooth nobody realized they'd been schooled in liberation.

The brahmins didn't know what to do with them. Here was someone who could quote scripture better than their best scholars but treated ancient texts like hot gossip, leaning in close to whisper "But did you catch the subtext though?" They'd show up to philosophical debates looking relaxed as a cat in sunlight, then systematically dismantle arguments that had stood for centuries, all while radiating enough lovingkindness to make the losers feel blessed about being proved wrong.

Their method was giving spiritual personal trainer energy - they knew exactly what each person needed and served it with devastating accuracy. For the angry ones: patience so deep it made the ocean look shallow. For the lazy: discipline wrapped in enough humor to make the medicine go down smooth. For the messy: ethical clarity sharp enough to split karma into its component parts. They met everyone exactly where they were, then casually showed them where they could be.

In the royal court's inner chambers, where power dressed itself in silk and whispers, they moved like someone who'd read the script of reality and found it amusing but ultimately unconvincing. Moving beyond any gender the court could name, hit the royal harem and there they were. Showing the girls exactly what power looked like when you owned it yourself. When you claimed it.

The courtesans recognized real power when they saw it—not the borrowed authority of titles or the temporary influence of beauty, but something that radiated from within like light through alabaster. They'd catch Vimalakirti's eye sometimes and see recognition there: both of them playing roles, but only one of them still believing in the performance.

But here's the thing about Vimalakirti—everything was choreographed, down to the way afternoon light caught their glass of water and turned it momentarily into liquid wisdom. They were laying down foundations more intricate than temple carvings, each interaction a brush stroke in a masterpiece most people wouldn't see until it was finished. When they helped that merchant calculate their profits, three other shopkeepers were watching. When they settled disputes in the marketplace, the crowd that gathered caught more than entertainment. Every move was a seed planted in soil they'd been quietly preparing for years.

So when word slipped out that Vimalakirti was feeling under the weather? Beloved, the response was giving season finale of your favorite prestige drama. The king's ministers came running like they'd heard enlightenment was on sale and supplies were limited. The merchants closed their shops early, for once not calculating the lost profit. Brahmins showed up with their scrolls, ready to take notes but trying to look casual about it. These weren't random spiritual tourists - these were people who'd watched Vimalakirti demonstrate truth in real time, who'd seen them handle gold like it was dust and treat street sweepers like kings.

They found Vimalakirti in their private chamber, which was doing that thing where space forgot it was supposed to behave like normal physics. The walls kept suggesting they continued into infinity while feeling more intimate than a whispered secret. Vimalakirti was reclining on a simple daybed that somehow made every throne in the palace look try-hard, their "illness" more precisely crafted than editorial fashion spreads.

The crowd pressed in close, silk robes rustling like prayers, jewelry clicking like nervous mantras. When the room was packed tighter than a temple on festival day, Vimalakirti adjusted their position—a movement small as a butterfly landing but it reset the energy of the entire room.

"Let me tell you about this body you're all so pressed about," they said, voice clear as temple bells despite their supposed weakness. "It's got the structural integrity of a dream about clouds. Less reliable than midnight promises, more high maintenance than a trophy spouse, and about as permanent as yesterday's weather."

The crowd leaned in closer. A young noble in the front row touched his expensive robes like he was checking if they'd turned to smoke.

"This body?" Vimalakirti continued, each word precise as acupuncture, "It's giving very that. Temporary realness. The kind of construction quality you get from a rushed renovation. Try to hold onto it? Like trying to grip air. Try to keep it pretty? Like painting on running water. It's under constant renovation but the contractors are all blind and working from different blueprints."

A merchant who'd spent that morning arguing over silk prices suddenly felt the weight of his rings like chains.

"We're out here treating these bodies like they're permanent addresses when they're more like cheap rentals. Adding luxury fixtures to a condemned building. Fighting over the feng shui of a sandcastle while the tide's coming in."

The silence in the room grew teeth.

"But let me tell you about a body worth investing in," they said, sitting up straighter as the teaching reached its peak. "The Buddha's body? That's the ultimate upgrade. Built from wisdom instead of proteins, structured with merit instead of minerals. The foundation? Pure ethics. The walls? Meditation. The roof? Wisdom that doesn't leak in the worst storms. And the decorations? Loving-kindness that never goes out of style. Compassion that doesn't wear out. Joy that doesn't depend on the weather. The kind of equanimity that keeps you waterproof against any drama."

In the crowd, understanding landed at different speeds, like rain on different surfaces. Some got it instant, like hot stone in a sudden shower. Others, it sank in slow, like water into dry earth. The court physician closed his diagnostic manual like closing the door on an empty house. A young priest touched his prayer beads then let them fall, realizing he was holding onto floaties in an ocean of meaning.

"Most of y'all," Vimalakirti continued, watching revelations bloom across faces like slow-motion flowers, "spend your mornings with your beauticians. Oils for the skin, powders for the face, gold thread for the robes - all that effort to decorate something that's already starting to fade before the paint dries." Their gaze caught a courtesan, who touched her carefully arranged hair then stopped, like she'd caught herself trying to fix a reflection in running water.

"But imagine spending that same time building something that doesn't fall apart. Each meditation session laying down another layer of unshakeable peace. Each act of kindness adding a room that thieves can't break into. Each moment of wisdom installing windows that look out on forever."

The late afternoon light did something complicated in the corners of the room, like reality was trying on different versions to see which one fit best. A baby started crying somewhere in the back, then stopped suddenly, caught by the sound of its own voice. The court physician, who'd been taking mental notes to diagnose Vimalakirti's condition, felt his professional skepticism dissolve like sugar in hot tea.

"You think I'm speaking in riddles?" Vimalakirti asked, addressing the unspoken doubts floating in the air like dust motes. "Tell me this - how many bodies have your medicines saved from death? How many face creams have stopped a single wrinkle from eventually having its way? We're out here treating symptoms while the real disease is our belief that any of this was meant to last."

A young merchant in the middle of the crowd—the kind of new money that wore its insecurities like oversized jewelry—cleared his throat. "And this... better body. I suppose it comes with a price tag? Special teachings for those who can afford them?" His voice carried a challenge, but underneath it trembled a desperate hope.

Vimalakirti's smile hit like sunlight finding diamonds in ordinary glass. "Already thinking about buying and selling, even here? No, Beloved. This transformation isn't for sale. Can't be bought, can't be sold, can't be stolen or lost. It starts with something simpler and harder than any transaction—seeing what's here, right now."

The merchant flushed darker than his expensive robes, but held Vimalakirti's gaze. Something was shifting behind his eyes, like furniture being rearranged in a room he'd thought he knew by heart.

The aging courtesan in the corner—still beautiful but aware of beauty's expiration date—spoke up, her voice carrying the weight of unasked questions. "But surely... some of us live in these bodies, depend on them. We can't all just..." She gestured at the air between them, where concepts like 'renunciation' and 'spiritual practice' hung unspoken.

"Look at me," Vimalakirti responded, their voice as temple incense. "Do I live outside the world? I've got a house that makes architects question their life choices. Family dynamics complex enough for a prestige drama series. I move through the marketplace and palace same as you. The difference isn't in what we do, but in how we hold it."

They shifted position again, the movement somehow suggesting both illness and perfect control. "The Buddha's qualities don't come from running away from life. They come from seeing it completely. From understanding that everything we're so pressed about—these bodies, these possessions, these reputations we're killing ourselves to maintain—they're all about as permanent as a social media trend."

The silence in the room grew roots.

"And yet," they continued, their voice warming like sun through stained glass, "this temporary body, this unreliable collection of elements constantly threatening to ghost us? It's also our chance. Like using a leaky boat to cross a river - not ideal, but if you bail water fast enough and steer smart, it'll get you to the other shore."

Understanding dawned at different rates across the crowd, like stars appearing in an evening sky. The merchant's hands had unclenched from their permanent grip on invisible account books. The courtesan's perfect posture had softened into something more real. Even the court physician had stopped trying to diagnose and started trying to understand.

The late afternoon light angled through windows that couldn't quite decide if they were rectangular or infinite. Someone's stomach growled, the sound earthly and perfect. The baby in the back of the room had fallen asleep, dreaming whatever dreams come to those not yet convinced they're separate from everything.

And through it all, Vimalakirti watched with eyes that held centuries of patience. This was the real miracle. Not instant enlightenment with special effects, but the slow turn toward truth, one heart at a time, one moment at a time. In a room full of people who came for a performance and found instead a mirror, showing them both the beautiful disaster of what they were and the impossible possibility of what they could become.

Outside, the mango trees leaned closer to the windows, their leaves whispering ancient secrets in a language made of sunlight and shadow. Inside, reality continued to behave strangely around the edges, like a painting starting to realize it wasn't bound by its frame. And in the space between, something shifted, adjusted, transformed. As invisible but as real as the moment between sleeping and waking, between winter and spring, between what was and what could be.

The crowd would leave soon, return to their markets and courts and temples. But they'd go differently. Moving a little lighter, seeing a little clearer, holding on a little less tightly to things that were always meant to flow through their hands like water, like light, like time itself.

4

Everyone Had Their Excuses Ready

There Miss Vimalakirti was, laid out on their fainting couch like Tennessee Williams wrote their entrance. One arm draped across the forehead in a pose that somehow managed to be both completely extra and absolutely authentic.

"The audacity," they muttered to the ceiling, which had started doing that thing where it revealed glimpses of other realms between the water stains. "Here I am, giving sick queen realness, and Buddha—that fully awakened, totally enlightened icon of icons—hasn't even sent a text. Not a 'you good, sis?' Not even a prayer hands emoji."

But Buddha, being Buddha (which is to say, being everyone and everything while making it look effortless), caught that shade before it even had time to throw itself. They turned to Sariputra, who was arranging their robes like they were trying to win Project Runway: Enlightenment Edition, and said with infinite gentleness, "Darling, why don't you go check on Vimalakirti?"

The look Sariputra gave Buddha could have stripped paint off a temple wall. "Oh no no no, not today Buddha! I'm still in recovery from the last time that queen read me for filth."

Sariputra's hands started moving like they were conducting an orchestra of memories. "There I was in the Great Forest, having my meditation moment under this tree that was serving thousand-year-old wisdom realness, feeling very that. Miss Thing comes strutting up, does the whole traditional head-to-feet greeting, proper as Sunday dinner at your grandma's—then proceeded to demolish my entire meditation technique like it was a clearance rack at TJ Maxx."

The air around Sariputra's head sparkled with the echoes of that dragging: "'Honey,'" they mimicked, their voice carrying every note of Vimalakirti's elegant devastation, "'this is NOT how we meditate in this house. You want to serve enlightened realness? Stop trying to hide your body and mind from the three realms like they're last season's mistakes. That's some basic queen energy right there. You need to maintain that deep meditative state while working the spiritual runway.'"

The memory was so strong it left traces in the air like cosmic lipstick marks. "'Don't be out here giving up your spiritual accomplishments while pretending to be like everybody else. Keep your mind from getting stuck on the inside or scattered on the outside—that's the sweet spot, darling. And those messy views you're running from? Use them to work the factors of enlightenment like they're your backup dancers.'"

Buddha's smile contained multitudes, each one sparkling with infinite compassion and just a hint of "I told you so." They turned to Maudgalyāyana, who was already backing away like someone who'd spotted their ex at Whole Foods.

"Not it!" Maudgalyāyana's hands went up faster than praise at a Baptist revival. "Let me tell you about the time I was in the town square, thinking I was serving wisdom realness to these householders. Had my dharma all laid out, presentations skills on point, feeling very that. Then Vimalakirti showed up looking like enlightenment went to fashion week."

The memory painted itself in the air: Vimalakirti, elegant as sunrise, devastating as truth, teaching dharma like it was both the highest art and the most natural thing in the world. "'Girl,'" Maudgalyāyana quoted, each word carrying the weight of that public reading, "'the dharma is like the ultimate clean slate—no drama, no ego, no baggage from past lives or future fantasies. It's giving pure liberation realness. It's everywhere like WiFi, but you can't see it. No color, no shape, no 'this is mine' nonsense. It's beyond your Instagram filters and your cognitive constructs.'"

And so it went, one after another, each disciple carrying their own story of being transformed by Vimalakirti's fierce wisdom. The air in Buddha's presence grew thick with memories: Mahakasyapa, Subhuti, Purnamaitreya, even young

Rahula and faithful Ananda, all of them marked by encounters that had left them humbled and elevated.

When Jagatindhara spoke, his memories painted themselves across the afternoon:

"Let me tell you about the time Māra came to my house in full divine drag - we're talking Indra realness that could have fooled the gods themselves. There I was, minding my spiritual business, when this vision appears with twelve thousand heavenly dancers who moved like they'd invented grace before the universe knew what to do with it.

"Māra was serving celestial elegance from every angle—gown that looked like dawn had decided to take fashion lessons from twilight, contouring that could reshape reality, and an aura that hit every divine note perfectly. These dancers? They made the apsaras look like they were at their first rehearsal. We're talking choreography that could rewrite the laws of physics.

"So Māra, thinking they'd nailed this Indra impersonation, tries to gift me these dancers like they're party favors. 'Here,' they said, voice dripping ambrosia, 'accept these beings as your servants.' And I'm sitting there thinking something's not quite right with this blessing, so I say, 'Thanks but no thanks—not exactly appropriate for this Buddhist boy.'

"That's when Vimalakirti appeared. And honey, let me tell you about an entrance. Didn't need special effects or backup dancers. Just stepped into reality like they owned it and said, 'Girl, please. This isn't Indra—this is Māra in drag trying to serve deception realness!'

"Then Vimalakirti turns to Māra and says 'Since these dancers aren't right for him, why don't you give them to me?' Māra tried to vanish. You know how demons do when they've been clocked. But couldn't move an inch. And this voice comes down from above, sounding like every authority figure who ever had to tell you to do something you didn't want to do: 'Hand. Them. Over. Then you can go.'

"Māra, shaken and stirred, had to give up those dancers. Without missing a beat, Vimalakiriti started teaching them about the nature of reality. 'Welcome to the house of dharma,' they said. 'Let's talk about a different kind of pleasure—the kind that sets you free instead of keeping you bound.'

"Māra started getting desperate, tries to call them back: 'Girls, let's go.' But they'd already caught the enlightenment bug. 'New spiritual path, who dis?'

"And Māra tried to get shady about attachment and possession, Vimalakirti said 'Take them! May they help every being find their truth!'

"Before they left, those dancers asked Vimalakirti how to serve enlightenment while still living in Māra's house. That's when we got 'The Inexhaustible Lamp' teaching: 'One lamp lights thousands without dimming - that's how wisdom works. The more you share it, the brighter it burns. You can live in the realm of illusion while still showing others the way out. That's how you pay it forward in the dharma game.'

The entire scene painted itself across the afternoon like a fresco artist had gotten their hands on stardust and decided to show off, each detail more vivid than the last, right down to the way Vimalakirti had clocked the divine masquerade with a single raised eyebrow that contained enough wisdom to fill a thousand sutras.

Buddha watched it all with the patience of someone who'd seen every possible version of this story play out across infinite universes. Each refusal was its own kind of tribute, each story a testament to how thoroughly Vimalakirti had mastered the art of teaching through divine shade.

Finally, there was Sudatta, still wearing the emotional equivalent of scuff marks from his charity gala reading. His story shimmered in the air like designer pearls, each one containing universes of teaching about true giving. The memory of those pearls, split between the poorest souls in town and a Buddha in another universe, left traces of light that danced through the afternoon like spiritual fireflies.

Buddha's smile, watching all this unfold, contained every teaching ever given and every lesson yet to come. The cosmic shade of it all was, itself, the most perfect teaching—a demonstration of how wisdom, wrapped in fierce love and served with divine style, could transform every soul it touched.

"Well," he said, his voice carrying hints of both infinite compassion and divine amusement, "perhaps it's time to see what the bodhisattvas have to say about all this." The air itself held its breath, waiting to see who would be brave enough—or fabulous enough—to face Vimalakirti's legendary wisdom.

5

Reading Sickness For Filth

Buddha's eyes sparkled with something that might have been mischief. "Your turn to check on Vimalakirti," he told Manjusri, and everyone who was anyone in all realms of existence caught their breath.

Manjusri, the crown prince of wisdom whose voice could shatter illusions like glass, actually laughed. "That one? Last time they gave a teaching, reality had to reconstruct itself afterward. Their philosophical reads leave enlightened beings questioning their whole path. But with your blessing," he adjusted his robes like someone preparing for battle, "I'll see what wisdom they're serving today."

Word spread through Vaishali faster than gossip at a family reunion. Eight thousand bodhisattvas dropped their meditation cushions and came running. Five hundred disciples abandoned their alms rounds mid-bowl. Gods and goddesses fell from heaven to catch this show. The crowd that followed Manjusri made the city's biggest festival look like a quiet dinner party.

Meanwhile, Vimalakirti was staging their space like the cosmic director they were. "Manjusri's coming? Let's give them something to think about." With a gesture that bent reality, they emptied their entire mansion. Every stick of furniture, every precious artwork, every sign of worldly life - gone. Nothing remained but their sickbed, floating in a void that somehow felt more full than empty.

When Manjusri entered, the air itself held its breath. Vimalakirti smiled from their sickbed, a smile that could have unraveled physics. "Welcome! Though technically, you haven't come, and I haven't actually seen or heard you. Because when you really look at it, has anyone ever really arrived anywhere?"

"Oh, we're starting there?" Manjusri's eyes lit up like someone who'd been dealt a perfect hand. "True that—once you've really seen something, you can't see it again, because both you and it have changed. Everything's new every moment, which means nothing's coming or going at all."

They were just warming up.

Manjusri glanced around the emptied space, every missing object screaming its absence. "The Buddha's asking how you're holding up with this..." he gestured at Vimalakirti's supernatural illness, "situation."

"You want to know what's making me sick?" Vimalakirti's voice filled the empty room like smoke. "I'm sick because every being is sick. Their suffering flows through me like blood. Every parent who's ever sat up all night with a fevered Beloved knows what I mean - but imagine feeling that for every being in existence. That's the price of real compassion, Beloved. It's not a choice, it's a condition of having your eyes open."

The air in the room got thicker with each word. Manjusri nodded slowly, then gestured at the pristine emptiness around them. "Speaking of having eyes open - why's your house giving minimalist realness today?"

"Because all Buddha-realms are empty," Vimalakirti said, like they were explaining why water is wet.

"Empty how?"

"Empty of what we think makes them real. Empty of our assumptions. Empty of our need to make them something specific."

"And what makes them that kind of empty?"

"Emptiness itself makes them empty. The same way space makes room for everything by being nothing in particular."

Manjusri's smile lit up dark matter. "What's empty about emptiness itself?"

"Everything we build in our minds is empty—even our ideas about emptiness."

"Can we build emptiness itself?"

Vimalakirti laughed. "Girl, even that concept is empty! Emptiness can't empty emptiness—that's like trying to use a knife to cut itself."

The philosophical tennis match accelerated until the walls themselves vibrated with meaning. Every question left traces in the air like heat lightning. Every answer rewrote reality a little more.

When Manjusri asked about maintaining mindset through illness, Vimalakirti sat up straighter, their presence filling the empty room like music: "Look at your own mind when you're sick. Really look. You'll find there's no solid "you" that's sick—we're a collection of elements doing their dance. Body, feelings, thoughts—they're all temporary performers on an empty stage."

They gestured at their own apparently ill body. "Even seeing yourself as a solid thing is another kind of sickness. The cure? Let go of the myth of ownership. Drop the illusion of separation. See how everything shares the same empty nature. Like words in a dream, they work until you try to grab them."

Manjusri leaned forward. "How should we support someone who's spiritually sick?"

"Keep it real but gentle," Vimalakirti said, their voice softening. "Talk about impermanence, but don't push them to give up everything. Yes, there's suffering, but don't make them feel like escape is the only answer. Serve truth with a side of compassion. Meet them where they are, even if where they are is a mess."

The empty room hummed with tension as Vimalakirti delivered their finale: "Our domain is pure uniqueness. It's not for the basics or the cooked. We work in the world without drowning in its drama. We see through illusion but stick around to help others see too. We know the truth but don't spill all the tea at once."

Their voice dropped to a whisper that somehow filled the universe: "We manifest magic like it's nothing, read spiritual levels like a book, and clock the Buddha's powers while looking casual. We're enlightened but still make fine distinctions, walk the path while sidestepping the obvious traps, stay balanced without checking out completely."

Manjusri's smile had grown with each word. He'd come for a wellness check and walked into a masterclass on the nature of reality itself. Through it all, Vimalakirti reclined on their sickbed like it was a throne in space, every gesture writing liberation in the air, their presence making emptiness feel full.

The ultimate flex wasn't what they displayed, it was what they made disappear. Every concept, every assumption, every limited way of seeing the world vanished like mist in morning sun. In that empty room, truth hit different. Even the dust danced in understanding.

6

Inconceivable Liberation

Sariputra stepped into Vimalakirti's house like he was
walking into a riddle. The room sprawled before him,
vast as possibility itself, empty as a midnight sky waiting for
stars. Not a cushion, not a mat, not so much as a forgotten
throw pillow graced the gleaming floors that somehow held
reflections from every universe that ever dreamed itself into
being.

The space breathed with anticipation, and the
walls—well, they were having thoughts about whether they
wanted to remain walls at all. Light poured in from windows
that opened onto seven different versions of dawn, each one
spilling color across the floor.

"Where's everyone supposed to sit?" The question escaped
Sariputra's lips before his wisdom could catch it, tumbling
into the air like a pearl dropped on marble.

Vimalakirti, stretched out on a daybed that might have been carved from moonlight, fixed him with a look that could have taught mountains how to dance. "Did you come for the tea or the chairs, Beloved?" The words rolled out smooth as aged bourbon, each syllable carrying centuries of cosmic shade wrapped in velvet. "Because I promise you ain't ready for either."

The air in the room shifted, tasting suddenly of possibility. Sariputra, bless his earnest heart, drew himself up like right-eousness in silk robes. "Obviously for the teachings!" His voice carried that particular tone of someone who had just realized they were about to get schooled and was trying to pretend they'd planned it that way.

Vimalakirti's laugh rippled through reality like pebbles dropped in the ocean of time. "Oh honey, if you were really here for the dharma, you wouldn't be worried about your own body, let alone some chair! You're out here acting like your physical form is the main character when it's barely even a supporting role."

The walls leaned in to listen, and somewhere in the dis-tance, a galaxy paused its spinning to take notes.

"True spiritual seekers aren't caught up in all that material drama—physical sensations, thoughts, consciousness, none of it! Y'all are out here treating liberation like it's something you can add to cart and get next-day shipping on."

Vimalakirti's words began painting themselves in light across the air, each truth materializing like celestial graffiti. "The real tea is that dharma is pure peace. Not the kind you can post about, not the kind you can hashtag. It's what's left when you stop trying to make everything into something."

The room itself exhaled, and in that breath, five hundred celestial beings who had been playing it cool in the upper atmosphere suddenly got it. Like, really got it. The kind of getting it that turns your entire existence into one long "oh."

"Listen," Vimalakirti continued, each word now dropping into reality like seeds that sprouted instant enlightenment, "dharma isn't about attachment, even to liberation. It's not something you can grab or clock. It's not your safety blanket or your spiritual aesthetic. It's beyond your little labels and categories. Stop trying to make dharma happen - it's not a thing you make happen, it's the happening itself."

Turning to Manjusri, who had been radiating wisdom from the corner like the universe's best-kept secret, Vimalakirti asked, "You've been everywhere, crown prince of cosmic realness—where's the best throne setup you've seen?"

Manjusri, eternal youth glowing like tomorrow's sunrise, leaned forward as if sharing gossip that could reshape galaxies. "If you sashay east past like billions of universes—and I do mean billions, honey, not Instagram billions but real cosmic billions—there's this place called Merudhvaja. The Buddha there, Merupradīparāja, is serving giant realness. I'm talking 84,000 leagues tall with a throne to match. The kind of throne that makes other thrones look like discount furniture."

That's when Vimalakirti decided to show all the way out. With a gesture that somehow managed to be both casual and capable of rearranging reality's source code, they manifested thrones. Not just any thrones—we're talking thrones that made the Iron Throne look like a folding chair at a community center. These weren't pieces of furniture; they were manifestos of majesty, dissertations on divine right, entire philosophical treaties carved in light and possibility.

The laws of physics took one look at what was happening and decided to call in sick for the day. The room, which should have been stuffed fuller than a Southern grandmother's Tupperware cabinet after Thanksgiving, somehow remained spacious as infinity itself. Each throne found its perfect place in space-time, like they'd always been there, just waiting for someone to notice.

"Take a seat, Beloveds!" Vimalakirti called out, voice smooth as butter on warm cornbread. The advanced practitioners transformed themselves with the ease of changing Instagram filters, but the baby bodhisattvas stood there looking like they'd been asked to explain quantum physics to a goldfish.

Sariputra, still hovering by the door like uncertainty wearing designer robes, gave the thrones the kind of look usually reserved for complicated restaurant menus. "These thrones are... a lot," he managed, his voice carrying all the confidence of a penguin at a phoenix convention.

"Just bow to Buddha Merupradīparāja, Beloved, and watch what happens," Vimalakirti advised, smooth as silk in still water. When they did, suddenly they were working those thrones like they were born to it, like celestial royalty at the universe's most exclusive gala.

"How?" Sariputra breathed, wonder replacing worry in his voice. "How are you fitting all this in your tiny house without disrupting the entire universe?"

Vimalakirti's smile taught stars how to shine. "It's called 'inconceivable liberation,' sweetie - and that's not just a fancy title. We're talking about the kind of power that lets a queen stuff Mount Everest in a mustard seed without changing either one's size. The kind of mastery that means you can pour entire oceans into a single pore without disturbing a single fish's afternoon nap."

The air in the room began to sparkle, each speck of dust telling its own story of transformation. "This liberation lets you play with time like it's your personal playlist—making weeks feel like eons or eons feel like weeks, depending on what beings need for their awakening. You can showcase all the fierce looks of every Buddha realm in one spot, hold all beings in your palm like they're precious gems, serve every offering ever given to any Buddha through a single pore, and still not have a hair out of place."

Mahākāśyapa, looking like wisdom wrapped in sunset clouds, stood up then. His voice carried the weight of mountains and the warmth of summer rain. "We, the regular disciples, have been like blind queens at the cosmic ball, thinking we knew how to dance when we barely knew where the dance floor was. Any being with a spark of wisdom would do well to throw themselves into this vision, this path to Buddhahood that's wider than the sky and deeper than forever."

His words lit up the room like spiritual fireworks, and 32,000 celestial beings suddenly found themselves reaching for enlightenment like it was the last piece of sweet potato pie at the family reunion.

Vimalakirti wasn't done though. The truth was flowing now. "Those demons you see causing drama across the universes? Baby, those are enlightened queens in disguise, serving tough love realness to help beings grow. And all those beings coming for the bodhisattvas' possessions, body parts, kingdoms, and relationships? That's just advanced bodhisattvas testing their sisters' commitment to the path."

The room itself nodded in agreement, walls swaying like trees in a cosmic wind. "Regular folks don't have the range to challenge bodhisattvas like that unless they're given permission. It's like comparing a dollar store glow stick to the sun, or a basic donkey trying to come for a fierce elephant. Regular folks can't touch these enlightened queens unless they're allowed to."

The very air shimmered as Vimalakirti continued, each word carrying the weight of centuries yet floating light as dandelion seeds on a summer breeze. "Only bodhisattvas can truly read other bodhisattvas, Beloved. Only they can clock that level of divine shade. That's the power of inconceivable liberation—not just bending reality, but understanding why it needs to bend."

A soft golden light began to pool in the corners of the room, thick as molasses and bright as truth. It crept up the walls like dawn climbing a mountain, touching everything with the kind of radiance that makes shadows look enlightened. The assembled beings watched in awe as each surface it touched began to tell its own stor—tales of countless lives, countless deaths, countless moments of awakening.

"You want to know what real power looks like?" Vimalakirti's voice dropped to a whisper that somehow filled the universe. "It's not about moving mountains or walking on water. It's about seeing the perfect stillness at the heart of every storm, the silence between every heartbeat, the peace that dances in the spaces between your thoughts."

The thrones, which had been quietly demonstrating advanced geometric theories about the nature of space-time, began to hum in harmony with these words. Each note carried the essence of a different Buddha realm, weaving together into a symphony that sounded like what enlightenment might taste like if you could pour it into a crystal glass.

"Every being you meet," Vimalakirti continued, gesturing with a grace that left trails of starlight in the air, "is either a teacher in disguise or a student waiting to discover they're actually a teacher. The universe isn't just a stage. It's a classroom, a temple, and the most exclusive cosmic salon all rolled into one."

Sariputra found his voice. "But how do we... how can we possibly..."

Vimalakirti's laugh rolled through the room like thunder wrapped in silk. "You're still trying to solve enlightenment like it's a math problem, aren't you? Still looking for the spiritual equivalent of a step-by-step tutorial?" The words danced in the air, each one trailing sparkles of divine truth. "The path isn't about getting somewhere else – it's about realizing where you've been all along."

As if to demonstrate this point, the room began to slowly rotate on an axis that shouldn't have existed, revealing layers of reality stacked like the pages of a book. Through each layer, the assembled beings could see different versions of themselves—some enlightened, some struggling, some figuring out which way was up.

"The real gag is," Vimalakirti said, every word now blooming into lotus flowers that floated through the impossible space, "that everything you're looking for is already right here. Every truth you're chasing has been waiting patiently for you to stop running long enough to notice it's been holding your hand the whole time."

The assembled beings sat in a silence so profound it had its own flavor, like your grandmother's best kept secret. Even the air was holding its breath, waiting to see what reality would do next.

Mahākāśyapa, looking like wisdom had decided to try on human form to see how it fit, leaned forward. His robes whispered against the throne like autumn leaves discussing philosophy. "All this time," he said, voice rich as dark soil after rain, "we've been treating enlightenment like it's some far-off city we need directions to reach. But it's more like trying to find the ocean while swimming in it."

The light in the room shifted again, this time moving like slow honey through crystal, revealing layers upon layers of truth stacked like the years in an ancient tree. Each layer showed a different version of reality – here a world where thoughts manifested as butterflies, there a realm where wisdom took the form of dancing rain, beyond that a dimension where silence had color and peace had texture.

"That's exactly it," Vimalakirti said, their voice carrying echoes of every teaching ever whispered under every bodhi tree that ever grew. "We're not trying to get anywhere new. We are trying to arrive where we've always been. It's not about adding something to yourself. It's about noticing what was never missing."

As if to illustrate this point, the thrones began to slowly dissolve, not into nothingness but into understanding. Each one melted like a metaphor coming true, revealing that what had seemed solid was made of pure light. The assembled beings found themselves supported by nothing but wisdom itself, floating in a space that was vast as infinity and intimate as a heartbeat.

"You see?" Vimalakirti gestured to the transformation happening around them, their movement leaving trails of enlightenment in the air like calligraphy. "Even these grand thrones, these magnificent displays of divine power—they're just temporary arrangements of truth trying on different forms. The real throne is the wisdom that sees through all forms to the empty clarity at their heart."

The room, which had already been playing fast and loose with the concepts of space and dimension, now began to demonstrate what infinity looks like when it decides to dance. Walls became windows into other realms, the ceiling opened onto views of a thousand different kinds of sky, and the floor revealed depths that went all the way down to the foundation of reality itself.

"The universe," Vimalakirti continued, "is not just vaster than you imagine, Beloved—it's vaster than you can imagine. And yet, every bit of that vastness, every galaxy, every atom, every moment of time itself, fits in the space between your thoughts."

The assembled beings watched as reality continued its elegant restructuring, each shift revealing new layers of truth like pages. Some of the younger bodhisattvas were taking notes with pens that wrote in pure light, their observations causing small explosions of understanding wherever ink met air.

"You want to know?" Vimalakirti asked, their voice carrying both the weight of mountains and the lightness of dawn. "Every single being in every single realm is already a Buddha. They're wearing confusion like it's the latest fashion trend, thinking their temporary costumes are their true nature."

As if responding to these words, the air itself began to crystallize into mirrors—not the ordinary kind that show you your face, but the divine kind that reflect your original nature. Each mirror caught and held a different aspect of truth:

here the emptiness that fills every form, there the compassion that moves through all things like wind through leaves.

"Look at yourselves," Vimalakirti commanded, though their voice was soft as twilight. "Really look. Past the roles you're playing, past the stories you're telling, past even your most cherished ideas about who and what you are."

The mirrors shifted and spun, creating a kaleidoscope of revelation. In one reflection, Sariputra saw himself as laser light. In another, he was a constellation of questions slowly transforming into answers. In a third, he existed as nothing but awareness, watching the play of phenomena like a grandmother watching Belovedren at play—with perfect love and perfect detachment.

"This is why the demons can't touch us unless we allow it," Vimalakirti continued, drawing patterns in the air that became new laws of physics. "This is why no challenge can overwhelm us unless we agree to be overwhelmed. When you know what you are—not just intellectually, but in your bones, in your breath, in the spaces between your heartbeats—then every obstacle becomes an invitation to demonstrate truth."

The room, which had been relatively well-behaved for a space that was actively transcending the laws of reality, now began to demonstrate what happens when infinity decides to be its full grown self. Corners opened onto other dimensions, the ceiling became a floor for higher realms, and the walls rippled with possibilities that mathematics hadn't invented equations for yet.

"Every moment," Vimalakirti said, their words now planting gardens of understanding in everyone who heard them, "is a door to liberation. Every breath is an opportunity to remember your true nature. Every challenge is the universe asking you to recognize yourself in a new way."

Five hundred celestial beings, who had been watching this display with increasing recognition, suddenly burst into light like stars remembering they were made of fire. Their awakening sent ripples through reality that caused enlightenment flowers to bloom in a thousand different realms.

7

The Goddess

Manjusri, eternal youth glowing like tomorrow's promise, turned to Vimalakirti with a question that sparkled with hidden depths. "How should a bodhisattva read other beings?" The words hung in the air like crystals catching light from a thousand suns.

Vimalakirti's response came wrapped in truth: "Like reflections dancing on water when the moon is full and feeling philosophical. Like magic tricks that got their master's degree in illusion. Like mirror images having an identity crisis." Their voice dropped to a whisper that somehow filled the universe, "All that glitters isn't gold, honey—and even gold isn't gold when you look close enough."

The air in the room began to demonstrate these metaphors in real time, reality rippling like a pond disturbed by truth. "They're like mirages serving their best oasis fantasy, echoes playing telephone with emptiness, clouds writing poetry in the sky—here for a moment, gone the next, never quite as solid as they think they are."

Manjusri, light trailing from his fingers like wisdom made visible, pressed deeper: "If everything's such an illusion, how do you still serve love? How do you keep that heart open when you know it's all smoke and mirrors?"

Vimalakirti's smile taught stars new ways to shine. "By wanting everyone to get their spiritual glow-up! That's the kind of love that's real—no drama, no thirst, no delusion. We're talking diamond-hard love that can't be broken, pure as fresh snow before the world writes its stories on it."

The walls of the room began to pulse with this teaching, each surface becoming a demonstration of what true love looks like when it takes physical form. "It's that enlightened love that wakes people up from their spiritual naps, spontaneous and authentic—not that fake influencer kind that's all filters and no substance."

The dialogue continued, each question and answer causing reality to shift and reshape itself in demonstration:

"What's a bodhisattva's compassion?" The question rang out like a bell calling universes to prayer.

"Giving away all your good karma to others," Vimalakirti responded, their words creating ripples of light that touched everyone present with the essence of true giving.

"What's their joy?"

"Living to give without regrets—the kind of joy that makes the sun look like it's still learning how to shine."

"What's their equanimity?"

"Whatever helps everyone—and honey, sometimes that help comes dressed as a challenge."

Just then, like divine timing had decided to show off its perfect choreography, a goddess materialized in their midst. She wasn't just invisible—she was wearing transparency like it was haute couture, existence itself turned into the season's hottest look. Gagged by the wisdom being served, she showered everyone with flowers that weren't just flowers but tiny manifestations of truth in bloom.

The flowers, each one a lesson in impermanence dressed up in petals, did something curious: they slid right off the bodhisattvas like water off cosmic duck feathers, but stuck to the disciples like spiritual post-it notes they couldn't quite shake.

The goddess, catching Sariputra in his flower-shaking struggle, delivered her first read of the evening: "Why you mad, sis?"

Sariputra, still trying to dignify his way out of a flower shower, protested: "These aren't appropriate for spiritual people." Every word came out accompanied by a flutter of petals that seemed to be critiquing his argument.

The goddess wasn't having it. Her truth came wrapped in divine shade: "The flowers are fine, child. They don't judge—they're out here being their authentic selves. You're the one with all the hangups! The real inappropriate thing is all your mental drama about what's proper and what's not! Notice how these flowers aren't sticking to the bodhisattvas? That's because they're not caught up in their heads like you are. Just like ghosts can't scare someone who isn't afraid, worldly things can't mess with someone who's truly free."

The air itself snapped in appreciation of this truth, and somewhere in the distance, a constellation rearranged itself to better catch the show.

Sariputra, trying to change the subject like someone switching playlists at an awkward moment, asked: "How long have you been here?"

The goddess's response came quick as lightning dressed in silk: "As long as you've been 'liberated.'" Each word dripped with irony, making quotation marks in the air with light.

"So... a while then?" Sariputra ventured, his dignity trying to find its footing on increasingly metaphysical ground.

"You tell me—how long have you been 'free'?" The goddess's words turned the air into mirrors, each one reflecting a different kind of freedom that Sariputra hadn't quite claimed yet.

Silence fell like velvet through starlight. Sariputra, whose wisdom usually flowed like a river, found himself suddenly contemplating the profound nature of keeping quiet.

The goddess, her very presence now teaching lessons about the nature of appearance and reality, wasn't about to let this teachable moment pass. "Aren't you supposed to be the wise one? The one whose understanding runs deeper than oceans? Why so quiet now? Did truth catch your tongue?"

Sariputra managed to find some words behind his enlightEmmett: "Liberation isn't measured in time. It's a complete transformation of..." His voice faltered as he caught himself falling into lecture mode.

"Here I go again," he thought to himself, "reaching for philosophical explanations when faced with direct challenge."

Aloud, now with new humility, he said, "Perhaps... perhaps I'm not as free as I thought. Each moment like this reveals new layers of subtle attachment."

Goddess: "At least that answer has a touch of truth in it."

"Every syllable you speak is liberation itself!" The goddess's laugh caused flowers to bloom in seven different dimensions. "Don't act like you have to stop talking to be free. True liberation is seeing everything as equal, period! The silence and the speech, the profound and the profane, the sacred and the silly. It's all one cosmic dance."

Trying to regain his philosophical footing, Sariputra reached for traditional teaching like a security blanket: "Isn't liberation about dropping desire, hate, and delusion?"

The goddess snapped her fingers, and reality rearranged itself to better hear her response: "That's the basic package for the spiritually entitled. The real queens know those things ARE liberation. The poison IS the medicine, if you've got the wisdom to transform it."

"WERK!" Sariputra exclaimed, surprising himself with his enthusiasm. "What's your secret?"

The goddess's smile taught diamonds new ways to sparkle. "No secret, no achievement. That's why I can speak truth. Anyone claiming achievements is just being extra. When you've got nothing to prove, everything proves itself."

The room began to demonstrate this teaching, each surface becoming more real and more transparent, like reality deciding to show all its cards at once. The walls breathed wisdom, the floor flowed like liquid light, and the ceiling opened onto views of truth that mathematics hadn't invented numbers for yet.

"Which path are you on?" Sariputra asked, his curiosity overwhelming his dignity. "Disciple, Solitary, or Great Vehicle?"

"Oh honey," the goddess replied, her words painting mandalas in the air, "I serve whatever's needed—basic teachings for beginners, interdependence for intermediates, and that Great Vehicle fantasy for everyone because we all need that ultimate liberation. It's like having a cosmic wardrobe—you wear what fits the occasion, but you don't get attached to any particular outfit."

She gestured around the room, which obligingly began to showcase its wonders like the universe's most exclusive spiritual boutique. "Living in this house is like being at the most fabulous spiritual spa—you can't smell anything basic when you're surrounded by Buddha realness. Even the celestial beings who visit get their lives and start living for enlightenment. The transformation is real, child, and it's spectacular."

Light pooled in her hands as she began counting off the house's wonders, each word creating ripples in reality that demonstrated her points. "I've been here twelve years, child, and haven't heard a single basic teaching—just pure love, compassion, and fierce Buddha qualities served fresh daily."

The air itself began to crystallize around her words as she enumerated the eight wonders, each one manifesting as she spoke. "This house has eight wonders, honey, and let me tell you about them. First, there's this constant golden light that makes the sun and moon look basic—the kind of radiance that has other lights questioning their career choices."

As if on cue, the room filled with a light that came from everywhere and nowhere, making even shadows look luminous. "Second, your drama disappears the moment you walk in—and I mean all of it, not the surface stuff. Third, we get constant visits from celestial royalty and bodhisattvas from every realm, it's the universe's most exclusive spiritual salon."

The walls rippled in agreement, briefly becoming transparent to reveal glimpses of other realms where beings of light went about their enlightened business. "Fourth, the house is always serving dharma talks about transcendence—not your basic 'be good' lectures, but the real cosmic tea about the nature of reality itself."

Music began to flow through the space, each note carrying teachings too profound for words. "Fifth, there's a constant soundtrack of divine music spilling Buddhist truth. Every beat drops wisdom, every melody reveals emptiness."

The floor beneath them became transparent, revealing endless treasures that sparkled with both material and spiritual wealth. "Sixth, we have these endless treasure chests full of jewels that anyone can use without them running dry. Abundance without attachment, wealth without worry."

The ceiling dissolved into a kaleidoscope of Buddha-fields, each one hosting its own enlightened being sharing wisdom. "Seventh, all the major Buddhas pop in for guest appearances to spill the real tea about enlightenment. And eighth?" She gestured, and the entire house became a living demonstration of divine possibility, "This house reflects all the fierce looks of every divine realm and Buddha field. Who could settle for basic teachings after seeing all this?"

Sariputra, still processing this display of cosmic fabulousness, tried to regain some traditional ground. "Why don't you transform out of your female form?" The words had barely left his mouth before they started looking embarrassed about their own existence.

The goddess's laugh caused reality to ripple like silk in a divine wind. "Oh, child. I've been looking for this 'female form' for twelve years and still can't find it. If someone conjured a woman with magic, would you ask her the same thing?"

"No," Sariputra admitted, "because she wouldn't really exist..."

"Exactly!" The goddess's words created fireworks of understanding in the air. "Nothing exists the way we think it does. So why ask about changing something that's an illusion?"

Then she did THAT—the kind of move that makes enlightenment pause to take notes. With a gesture that bent reality like light through crystal, she switched their forms. Suddenly, Sariputra found himself serving goddess realness while she wore his form like it was haute couture.

"How's it feel to be 'female,' honey?" she asked in his own voice, each word carrying enough divine shade to cool a thousand summer afternoons.

Sariputra, now rocking a whole new perspective on existence, was shook. The universe itself leaned in, waiting for his response.

The goddess, still wearing his form like she'd been born to it, wasn't done with the lesson. "If you could change back, all women could change. But the Buddha already spilled the tea—in reality, there's no male or female. These are just costumes we're wearing in the cosmic play."

With another gesture that made geometry reconsider its life choices, they returned to their original forms. "What happened to your female form?" she asked, each word a flower blooming in the garden of understanding.

"I didn't make or change it," Sariputra replied, wisdom starting to dawn like a sun that had been hitting snooze on enlightenment.

"Exactly! Nothing is made or changed—that's the Buddha's truth, served hot and fresh for those ready to sip it."

The conversation continued, reality bending around their words like light around a black hole of understanding:

"Where will you be reborn?"

"Wherever the Buddha's magical manifestations appear, child. I go where the teaching needs serving."

"But those don't get reborn!"

"Neither does anything else, sweetie. That's the whole point."

"When will you become a Buddha?"

"When you go back to being basic—which is never."

"That's impossible!"

"Exactly! Enlightenment stands on impossibility. Because it's impossible, no one attains it. That's what makes it real."

The air between them crackled with paradox and possibility. "But the Buddha said countless beings have become enlightened!"

"That's convention, honey. Buddhas transcend past, present, and future. But tell me—are you really an arhat?"

"Yes," Sariputra replied, finding his footing in emptiness, "because there's nothing to attain."

"Same with enlightenment—it exists because there's nothing to attain. The seeking is the finding, the question is the answer, and the path is the goal."

Vimalakīrti, who had been watching this entire exchange like a cosmic tennis match, finally served the ace: "This goddess has served billions of Buddhas, mastered spiritual powers, and can manifest wherever she wants to help beings. She's been that girl all along!"

The room itself applauded, reality rippling with appreciation for truth so perfectly served. In that moment, understanding bloomed like flowers in the garden of emptiness, and the space between thoughts began to laugh with the joy of recognition.

8

The Scenic Route

The scene unfolded like silk catching light. Manjusri and Vimalakirti found themselves wrapped in an intimate dialogue about the subtle art of walking the Buddha's path. Vimalakirti reclined against a collection of cushions, playing the role of invalid with theatrical precision while their razor-sharp intellect gleamed behind half-lidded eyes. Manjusri, wisdom incarnate yet unseasoned by experience, perched at Vimalakirti's bedside, his posture taut with the weight of seeking.

The air in the room buzzed with anticipation as other bodhisattvas and seekers leaned in, each word precious as dewdrops at dawn. Manjusri's voice carried a slight tremor as he asked the question burning in his chest: "How does a bodhisattva navigate this journey toward enlightenment?"

Vimalakirti's lips curved into a knowing smile as they answered with casual grace, "By taking the scenic route, darling.

The real lessons live in the meandering paths, the unexpected detours, and the company we keep along the way. That's where we learn to weave compassion with wisdom."

"What do you mean by scenic route?" Manjusri asked, his curiosity piqued.

Vimalakirti adjusted their position, their eyes sparkling with divine mischief. "Listen up," they began, each word precise as cut crystal. "A bodhisattva might look like they're living their messy reality, but they're doing it with pure intention in their heart. They'll walk through hell but stay pristine as fresh snow. They'll dance with chaos but keep their wisdom intact. When they mingle with jealous gods, they stay humble and authentic, no drama needed."

The room itself leaned closer as Vimalakirti continued, their voice rich with lived experience. "They dive deep in meditation but don't get lost in spiritual bypass like some cosmic recluse. They navigate desire but don't let it claim them. They might flash anger but harbor no hatred. They act confused while keeping their mind crystal clear. They might seem greedy but give everything away. Their life might look chaotic but they're keeping it precise, catching every subtle mistake and living that essential life."

Reality rippled as the teaching deepened: "They might seem shady, but they radiate compassion. Looking lazy but working with unmatched dedication. Seeming distracted but focused with perfect precision. They might sound clueless, but they've mastered both worldly and spiritual knowledge."

Each word painted pictures in the air as Vimalakirti elaborated: "They might appear artificial, their words and actions a performance, but they're simply adapting, meeting people where they are with a grace that dissolves barriers and invites growth. You might think they're playing games, but each move serves a purpose, guiding others through existence with elegance and skill. Every gesture carries a promise to help fellow travelers cross the river of life, ensuring no one navigates its currents alone."

The teaching flowed like water finding its level: "They handle all human complexities while remaining immaculate. They walk through temptation but understand the Buddha's teachings through direct experience. They act like students but teach unprecedented wisdom. They might look solitary but their compassion could fill universes."

Vimalakirti's voice took on a rhythmic quality: "They might look broke but they're wealthy in ways beyond counting. They might seem limited, but they emanate enlightened presence. They might look ordinary but they carry the Buddha's lineage in their cells. They show up looking fragile and disheveled, but their essence remains unshakeable and luminous. They act old and sick but they've conquered the root causes and death holds no power over them anymore."

"They moved through royal courts yet stayed unattached, remembering impermanence in each breath. They danced in palaces while maintaining inner silence, floating above the endless drama."

Vimalakirti's voice softened to a whisper that filled the room. "That's how a bodhisattva works it while following Buddha's path," they concluded, each word carrying perfect balance between wisdom and authenticity.

Then Vimalakirti turned to Manjusri with a gleam in their eye. "Tell me about the Buddha's family lineage. Keep it concise."

Manjusri's response flowed like water over stones: "The Buddha's family includes everything - all the complicated tangles, all the ignorance and craving, all the desire and aversion and confusion, all the misguided views, all the things that bind us, all our senses and consciousness, all the missteps, all the irritations, and all the harmful actions. In essence, the Buddha's family embraces every wrong view, every turbulent emotion, and every imperfect quality."

"Elaborate on that," Vimalakirti prompted, one eyebrow raised in elegant inquiry.

Manjusri leaned forward, his words gathering momentum: "Consider this - someone who's already achieved clarity and walks the path of supreme goodness can't generate that initial spark of perfect enlightenment. But someone still caught in life's complications, who hasn't glimpsed the absolute? They can experience that awakening.

"Imagine lotus flowers - they won't flourish on dry ground. They need murky waters to bloom. Similarly, enlightenment doesn't arise in those already free - it grows from the rich soil of our messy existence.

"You can't plant a seed in empty space - it requires earth to flourish. The Buddha's qualities don't develop in those who've transcended everything. They blossom in people still cycling through existence.

"Only when someone's ego reaches mountainous proportions can the seed of enlightenment take root and flourish. Like diving for precious pearls in ocean depths, you can't cultivate complete wisdom without immersing yourself in the depths of experience."

Sariputra sat nearby, his mind whirling as the implications crystallized. He leaned forward, his forehead creased with dawning realization.

"Well," he thought, his customary certainty wavering, "if that's accurate, then those of us who've already purified ourselves can never manifest these enlightened qualities. Even those who've committed the gravest acts retain the potential to transform and gradually awaken - but we Arhats who've already resolved our internal conflicts? We're at a dead end."

He shifted uncomfortably, the weight of understanding settling into his bones. A new metaphor surfaced in his mind: "Just as someone without physical desire holds no sway over sensual pleasures, those of us who've broken free from attachments have no influence over the Buddha's teachings and can't conceive of seeking these precious dharmas."

The irony settled around him like evening shadows. Sariputra's fingers traced invisible patterns on the ground as his thoughts spiraled to their inevitable conclusion: "Perhaps the ordinary beings deserve more recognition than the

Arhats - they can hear of the Buddha's magnificence and feel inspired to reach for perfect enlightenment, while we remain unable to grasp it. Even if we spent countless lifetimes hearing about the Buddha's incredible powers, fearlessness, and remarkable qualities, we could never generate that supreme aspiration."

This revelation left him silent, his previous certainty about the path dissolving like mist in morning light.=

Vimalakirti observed this inner turbulence and responded with verses that shimmered with both elegance and power:

"For pure-hearted warriors on the path, wisdom becomes their mother,
Skill and compassion flow as father's gifts with love,
Joy in awakening as their eternal partner,
While kindness cascades like morning's light from above.

Clear seeing and wisdom as cherished children,
Empty essence creates their sacred space,
Their complex emotions transform to devoted students,
Moving through existence with unfettered grace.

Perfect virtues gather as their family near,
Serving others becomes their sacred, endless call,
Teaching liberation rings out as their sweetest music,
Rising up as they watch illusions fall.

Freedoms form their meditation pool so deep,

Pureness illuminating the way ahead,
Their vehicle vast beyond all measuring,
Carrying them where ancient masters led.

Good qualities adorned them for the path they chose,
High purpose crowned their noble, winding way,
Pure living brought rewards beyond imagining,
As they guided others through night and day.

Clear knowing woke them - ever bright and aware,
Liberation sustained them like celestial wine,
Pure intention cleansed their very essence,
Until their inner light began to shine.

Having conquered their shadows both waking and sleeping,
    They emerged as champions unswayed by doubt,
    They mastered all forms of inner darkness,
    While awakening's banner they carried out.

Though cycles of existence lacked ultimate substance,
They chose their manifestations with skillful care,
Illuminating Buddha's realms with wisdom,
Bringing hope to those caught in despair.

They honored countless Buddhas with devotion pure,
While seeing all as one unbroken light,
Working through all worlds with perfect wisdom,

Until suffering faded into night.

They revealed all forms in fleeting moments swift,
Played tempter's games to show the higher way,
Displayed life's shifts and transformations,
Helping beings find clarity each day.

They showed how all things must pass and change,
Appearing in myriad forms to guide,
Mastering every skill to aid all beings,
Letting wisdom be their ride.

They appeared as luminous celestial beings,
Became medicine in moments of need,
Offered sustenance during times of famine,
Planting awakening's precious seed.

In violent ages they practiced loving-peace,
Leading millions to find their calm within,
Remaining centered in the greatest conflicts,
Teaching others where to begin.

They entered realms of torment by choice alone,
To aid those caught in suffering's snare,
Teaching liberation throughout all dimensions,
Spreading wisdom everywhere.

They displayed both pleasure and meditation deep,

While showing neither held final sway,
Became whatever others most needed,
Helping ignorance fade away.

They emerged as leaders, merchants, mystic guides,
Serving as treasure for those in need,
Before the proud they showed achievement's heights,
Then planted humility's sacred seed.

They stood before those gripped by terror,
Offering protection firm and clear,
Helped them ripen toward awakening,
Showing what wisdom could appear.

As realized ones with powers five they dwelt,
Establishing beings in peace profound,
Skillfully serving all who sought their guidance,
Till liberation's path was found.

Their practices and reach knew no boundaries,
With boundless knowing setting beings free,
Not even Buddhas speaking endless ages,
Could tell their virtues' entirety.

Who but the lost, hearing of this noble path,
This journey toward awakening's light,
Would not aspire to supreme enlightenment's goal,
And make this wisdom their delight?"

The verses hung in the air like strung pearls, each one reflecting infinite facets of the bodhisattva's path. The assembled beings sat in appreciative silence, letting the teaching settle into their awareness. Each word had carved new channels of understanding in their minds, like rain creating rivers in fertile soil.

Vimalakirti's eyes swept across the gathering, seeing how the verses had transformed the very atmosphere of the room. The teaching remained suspended between them all, not as mere words but as living possibilities, each listener glimpsing their own potential reflected in the mirror of these verses.

The moment extended, perfect in its completion, as the last echoes of the teaching rippled through countless realms of existence.

9

Non-Duality

Vimalakirti lounged on his sickbed like it was a throne, the walls stretching wider than physics should allow. The late afternoon light caught his smile - that knowing look your wisest auntie gave right before she changed your whole life with three sentences.

"Y'all," he said, voice soft but carrying straight to the bone, "tell me how a bodhisattva steps into non-duality. Each of you speak your piece."

The room got that special kind of quiet, like when somebody at the family reunion's about to spill tea that'll reshape the whole family tree. Every enlightened being in that impossibly large room started looking at each other like students when the professor asks the hardest question on the final.

Dharmavikurvana stood up first, straightening his robes like he was about to testify in church. "Birth and death look like opposites," he said, "but nothing was ever really born, so how could it die? Understanding that? That's non-duality."

Srigandha jumped in next, leaning forward like he was sharing gossip over coffee. "We stay stuck thinking 'me' and 'mine,' but baby, when you realize neither one exists? That's the moment right there."

The hits kept coming. Every bodhisattva had something to say about pairs of opposites dissolving into truth:

Good and bad? Just labels.

Pure and impure? Same thing from different angles.

Heaven and hell? Honey, please - they're the same zip code.

Body and mind? One dance, different moves.

World and transcendence? That line was drawn in water.

The room kept expanding with each truth dropped, like somebody was stretching reality like taffy. Every piece of furniture started remembering it used to be stardust.

Sariputra, being Sariputra, spoke up. "With respect, Vimalakirti, I've taught the doctrine of non-duality to hundreds of monks. Through logical analysis, we can demonstrate how apparent opposites resolve into unity. For instance, if we examine the nature of light and dark..."

Vimalakirti quipped, "And has this logical analysis freed you from duality?"

Sariputra paused, his scholar's confidence wavering. "I... I can explain the concept perfectly. My treatise on the subject is studied in three monasteries." His voice softens. "And yet, when faced with praise or blame, I still feel the pull of preference. Despite all my understanding, something remains distant between knowledge and realization."

Then Manjusri, looking fresh as Sunday service with wisdom trailing off him like designer perfume, sized up the crowd. "Y'all spoke truth," he said, "but talking about non-duality makes it dual. Real non-duality? That's when you don't say nothing about nothing."

Every eye in that infinite room turned to Vimalakirti like he was about to announce the winner of the cosmic talent show. "Your turn," Manjusri said. "Show us how it's done."

Vimalakirti just lay there, quiet as sunrise.

Not empty quiet. Full quiet. The kind of quiet that makes noise look shabby.

Manjusri's face lit up like Christmas. "Now THAT'S what I'm talking about!" he exclaimed. "When words tap out, that's where truth begins."

In that silence, five thousand beings got it. Really got it. The kind of getting it that changes everything forever.

The walls held that silence like a precious secret, while outside, Atlanta traffic flowed on, each horn honk suddenly sounding like the deepest truth ever told.

10

The Fragrant Feast

There was Sariputra, perched on the edge of his cushion, his mind churning like the wheels of an ancient cart stuck in the mud. "It's noon already," he mused inwardly, his gaze drifting towards the sun-drenched horizon beyond the assembly, "and these legendary Bodhisattvas are still serving dharma realness without so much as a water break. When are we going to eat?" His stomach growled, a soft protest that echoed through the silent grove, betraying his preoccupation with the mundane while celestial truths danced in the air.

"Even after all these years of practice, here I am, distracted by hunger. My teachers would be disappointed." He touched his begging bowl absently. "Yet wasn't it the Buddha himself who taught the middle way? Not too austere, not too indulgent..." His fingers trace the bowl's rim as memories surfaced. "Like that time when I lectured young monks about transcending bodily needs, only to faint from hunger during evening meditation. Buddha's gentle correction still echoes: 'Care for the vessel that carries wisdom.'"

He turned to a nearby monk and whispered, "Brother, do you ever find it curious? We spend years studying the deepest philosophical points, yet sometimes struggle with the most basic aspects of being human?"

Vimalakīrti, with a prescience as sharp as a diamond sutra, read Sariputra's mind with the ease of flipping through an open magazine on a lazy Sunday. He clocked that gnawing hunger, the subtle shift in Sariputra's energy, and with a knowing smile, he interjected, "Honey, didn't the Buddha teach you about the eight liberations? You should be focusing on those transcendent states, not obsessing about your next meal like you're waiting for the weekend brunch crowd to thin out. But if you're that hungry, wait just a hot minute. You're about to taste something that will make every meal you've ever had seem like those sad, wrinkled hot dogs spinning on a convenience store roller grill."

With this, Vimalakīrti's eyes twinkled with mischief, promising a revelation that would satiate a hunger far deeper than anything in the belly. Sariputra, caught between embarrassment and anticipation, could only swallow his pride along with his appetite, and wait.

Then Vimalakīrti entered into a fierce concentration - we're talking spiritual supermodel pose - and showed everyone a universe called Sarvagandhasugandhā (which meant "All The Best Smells, Darling").

To find this universe, you'd have needed to werk your way up through space, passing through more universes than there were grains of sand in forty-two Ganges rivers. That was where the Buddha Sugandhakūta lived his best life and taught his truth.

In this universe, the trees were serving fragrance fiercer than anything gods or humans could even dream of. The place was so elevated that words like "basic practitioner" or "solo enlightenment" weren't in their vocabulary—just pure Bodhisattva realness everywhere you looked. The Buddha Sugandhakūta had been teaching pure dharma to these advanced queens.

Everything in this universe - the viewing platforms, the meditation walkways, the gardens, the palaces, the clothes—was made of pure fragrance. And when that Buddha and his Bodhisattvas had eaten their food? The scent filled countless universes.

Right then, Buddha Sugandhakūta was having lunch with his Bodhisattva family, and this fabulous god named Gandhavyūhāhāra (serving "Arranged Fragrance Realness") had been waiting on them like the most attentive server at the most exclusive restaurant.

Back at Vimalakīrti's, everyone was gagging over this universe where Buddha Sugandhakūta and his Bodhisattvas were living their best fragrant lives.

Then Vimalakīrti had turned to the crowd and said. "Who's fierce enough to go snatch us some of that food?"

But thanks to Manjusri's supernatural shade, nobody could do it. Everyone just sat there, quiet as a meditation retreat.

Vimalakīrti had read Manjusri: "Girl, aren't you embarrassed for this assembly?"

Manjusri had clapped back: "Don't come for these Bodhisattvas like that. Didn't the Buddha say not to read advanced practitioners?"

Then Vimalakīrti, without getting up from his seat (because a queen knew how to werk from any position), had created an imaginary Bodhisattva that was giving pure gold realness. We're talking all the major and minor marks of enlightenment, serving looks so fierce they made everyone else look like they were wearing last season's robes.

Vimalakīrti told this fabulous creation: "Go up through all those universes, find the Sarvagandhasugandhā realm, and when you see Buddha Sugandhakūta, bow down and say: 'Vimalakīrti, living in the basic realm down below, sends his love and wants to know if you're feeling okay, if everything's good, if you're healthy and happy.' Then, after circling him mentally a hundred thousand times, ask if we could maybe get the leftovers from your meal? We're trying to help some spiritually hungry queens down here understand the Buddha's work. It'll help these basic practitioners develop some noble aspirations, and everyone will get to see how fierce the Buddha's qualities really are."

The imaginary Bodhisattva said "Yasss!" and sashayed away so fast none of the other Bodhisattvas saw them leave.

In a single moment, faster than you could say "enlightenment," they reached the Buddha Sugandhakūta and spilled all that tea exactly as instructed.

The Bodhisattvas up there were gagged by this stunning visitor and asked Buddha Sugandhakūta: "Where did this fierce queen come from? What's this Sahā universe they're talking about? And who are these basic practitioners they mentioned?"

Buddha Sugandhakūta explained: "If you go down through space, past as many universes as there are grains of sand in forty-two Ganges rivers, you'll find the Sahā universe. That's where Buddha Śākyamuni is working with beings who need extra help finding their spiritual path. That's also where Vimalakīrti lives, teaching inconceivable liberation to the Bodhisattvas there. He sent this imaginary queen to sing my praises and show off our universe to help develop those beings' potential."

Those Bodhisattvas were like: "This Vimalakīrti must be something else if he can create an imaginary being this powerful!"

Buddha Sugandhakūta spilled more tea: "Beloved, you don't know the half of it. This Bodhisattva sends imaginary beings to all ten directions, helping beings everywhere. In a single moment, he can create countless queens like this one and send them throughout the cosmos to serve the Buddha's work."

Then Buddha Sugandhakūta took some of that heavenly food—we're talking ambrosia realness, honey—and gave it to the imaginary Bodhisattva.

Ninety thousand Bodhisattvas up there were like: "Can we come too? We want to see Buddha Śākyamuni, pay our respects, and meet this Vimalakīrti person!"

Buddha Sugandhakūta said: "If you think it's the right time, go ahead. But listen up - when you get down there, tone down your fragrance. Those beings aren't ready for all that. Hide your beauty too, because you might make them feel some type of way. And whatever you do, don't get shady about their universe. Yes, it might look basic compared to ours, but remember - all Buddha-fields are fundamentally pure like space. The Buddhas show different versions to help different beings find their path."

So the imaginary Bodhisattva took that bowl of heavenly food and, with those ninety thousand Bodhisattvas, disappeared from the fragrant realm and appeared at Vimalakīrti's house faster than you could say "spiritual transformation."

Vimalakīrti created ninety thousand fabulous thrones for all these visitors, matching the ones already there. The imaginary Bodhisattva handed over that bowl of food, and honey, the fragrance! It filled the whole city of Vaishali and spread through thousands of universes.

In Vaishali, everyone from the brahmans to the basic householders caught that scent. The Licchavi chief named Candracchattra and his eighty-four thousand squad were gagged by the fragrance and immediately headed to Vimalakīrti's house.

When they saw all these Bodhisattvas on thrones so high and wide, they were shook. After paying their respects, they stood to the side like proper guests. Even the gods from every realm had shown up with their entourages, drawn by that heavenly aroma.

Then Vimalakīrti said to Sariputra and the other senior practitioners: "Come get this food, darling - it's divine ambrosia perfumed with great compassion. But don't come at it with any basic attitudes, or you won't be able to digest it."

Some of the less enlightened practitioners were looking at this food like "That's not enough for this crowd," but the imaginary Bodhisattva read them quick: "Don't measure this food by your limited understanding. The four oceans would dry up before this food runs out. Even if beings from countless universes took bites as big as Mount Sumeru for hundreds of lifetimes, this food wouldn't diminish. Why? Because it comes from inexhaustible spiritual qualities like ethics, meditation, wisdom, liberation, and the knowledge and vision of liberation."

Everyone ate and was satisfied, but the food hadn't run out. Those who had eaten it had felt the same bliss as Bodhisattvas in paradise, and their bodies had given off fragrances like the trees in that perfumed universe.

Then Vimalakīrti asked the visiting Bodhisattvas: "How does Buddha Sugandhakūta teach up there?"

They said: "He doesn't use words like we do down here. He teaches through pure fragrance. Under each perfumed tree sits a Bodhisattva, and when they smell these divine scents, they instantly get a spiritual concentration called 'Treasury of All Bodhisattva Qualities.' From that, all the Bodhisattva virtues naturally arise."

The visiting Bodhisattvas asked: "So how does Buddha Śākyamuni teach down here?"

Vimalakīrti said: "Girl, let me tell you - these beings down here need extra help. They're like unruly horses that need firm training. So Śākyamuni has to spell everything out:

This is hell, this is the animal realm, this is the ghost realm - here's what happens when you act messy.

This is bad body karma, this is bad speech karma, this is bad mind karma - and here's what you get for each one.

This is killing, stealing, sexual misconduct, lying, gossip, harsh words, useless chatter, greed, hate, wrong views - and here's what happens when you serve that kind of energy.

This is being stingy - here's what you get. This is being un-ethical - here's what you get. This is being angry - here's what you get.

Just like you need a strong prod to control wild horses and elephants, these beings need strong teaching about suffering to get them on the right path."

The visiting Bodhisattvas were shook: "Buddha Śākya-muni must be legendary to work with such difficult beings! He hides his fierce qualities and uses all these skillful methods to help them. And these Bodhisattvas who put up with all this mess? Their compassion is beyond!"

Vimalakīrti agreed: "That's right! And let me tell you something - the Bodhisattvas down here do more to help beings in one lifetime than y'all do up there in a hundred thousand lifetimes. Why? Because in this Sahā universe, we have ten powerful methods you won't find in other pure lands:

We help the poor through generosity

We help the messy through ethics

We help the angry through patience

We help the lazy through effort

We help the scattered through meditation

We help the confused through wisdom

We teach people how to avoid unfortunate rebirths

We introduce limited practitioners to the Great Vehicle

We help those without good karma create some

We constantly help beings through four methods of conversion

You won't find these ten dharmas in other pure Buddha-fields!"

The visiting Bodhisattvas had asked: "After leaving this basic realm, what qualities do we need to reach a pure land without getting read for filth?"

Vimalakīrti had served these eight conditions:

Help all beings without expecting anything back

Take on others' suffering and give them all your good karma

Stay unbothered and treat everyone equally

Live for other Bodhisattvas like they're your guru
Keep the faith in deep teachings you haven't heard before
Don't be jealous of others' gains or proud of your own
Check yourself before you wreck yourself, and help others calm their mess
Stay focused and collect all the good qualities

In a corner of Vimalakirti's ever-shifting chamber, where reality bent like silk in a divine breeze, Sariputra found himself seeking refuge in observation. The space around him breathed with possibilities, walls suggesting infinity while maintaining the intimacy of a whispered prayer. His gaze drifted across the assembly, each being radiating their own particular light, some bright as noon, others subtle as starlight through clouds.

A young monk approached, his steps as hesitant as his awakening faith. His robes, still stiff with newness, whispered against the floor that couldn't quite decide if it was marble or moonlight. The air between them held the particular tension of questions seeking their moment of birth.

"Venerable One," the young monk began, his voice carrying both reverence and that special kind of courage it takes to step into uncertainty, "might I intrude upon your contemplation with a question?"

Sariputra's smile carried echoes of the afternoon's lessons in humility. "Questions?" His voice held warmth enough to melt philosophical ice. "After today's teachings, I find myself increasingly uncertain about my qualifications to answer anything. Though perhaps that uncertainty itself qualifies me more than my previous certainty ever did." He gestured to the space beside him, the movement itself a teaching in welcome. "Please, ask."

"How do you maintain such grace when your understanding is challenged?" The words tumbled out like prayers from a broken mala. "When everything you believed solid starts feeling like mist in your hands?"

"Ah." Sariputra adjusted his robes with the precise movements of someone buying time to meet truth face to face. "Now that's a question I'm uniquely qualified to answer in this moment." The light catching his face held memories of a thousand debates, a hundred victories, and one transformative defeat. "Before I met the Buddha, they called me 'Upatissa the Wise.' The name carried weight in every philosophical circle from Rajagaha to the furthest reaches of the sixteen kingdoms. No debater could stand before me, no argument could withstand my analysis."

His eyes drifted toward Vimalakirti's resting place, where space itself seemed to hold its breath in perpetual anticipation. "But true wisdom, I'm discovering even now, isn't about having all the answers. It's about maintaining a heart open enough to always question, to always learn. The Buddha shared something with me once—" his voice softened like sunset deepening to dusk, "—that my greatest gift wasn't my celebrated intelligence, but my capacity to recognize truth when it appeared before me, even when that truth meant admitting everything I thought I knew was nothing but shadows and assumptions."

The air between them filled with understanding thick as incense, each breath carrying the perfume of ego dissolving into wisdom. Above them, the ceiling opened briefly onto views of truth that mathematics hadn't yet invented numbers to describe, while beneath them, the floor remembered it was nothing but space dressed in the illusion of solidity.

11

Unitl The Food's Digested

The Blessed Śākyamuni Buddha—OUR Buddha—was doing his thing in Amrapali's mango grove, serving dharma realness as usual, when suddenly the whole space started expanding like some divine gay club at peak hour. The assembly lit up with this fierce golden glow that had everyone gagged.

Ānanda, who never missed a beat, clocked this situation and was like, "Hold up, Blessed One - the grove's getting bigger and everyone's giving golden goddess lighting. Spill the tea."

The Blessed One smiled that knowing smile. "Oh honey, this is the preview. Vimalakīrti and Manjusri are about to make an entrance with their whole squad."

Next thing you know, Vimalakīrti's turning to Manjusri like, "Let's go see the Buddha, honey. Time to pay our respects and get that spiritual nourishment."

Manjusri, ever the composed, was like, "If you think it's time, let's work."

Then Vimalakīrti did something so extra—and I mean EXTRA extra. He straight up picked up the entire assembly, thrones and all, with his right hand like he was grabbing his morning coffee. Just snatched them all up and took them to where the Buddha was holding court. When they got there, he set everyone down like he was arranging flowers, bowed to the Buddha's feet seven times (because three times would've been basic), and stood to the side serving composed realness.

All those Bodhisattvas who'd come through from Buddha Sugandhakūta's universe got down from their thrones and did their thing—bowing, circling, the whole respectful fantasy. Those from our realm followed, and then all the celestial beings came through too, gods and guardians serving their best "we're not worthy" realness.

The Buddha gave everyone that warm welcome energy, letting them know they could take their seats, and everyone settled in like it was Sunday brunch.

Then the Buddha turned to Sariputra and was like, "Did you catch all that supernatural flexing from these Bodhisattva queens?"

Sariputra was like, "Yeah, and honestly? I can't even. Their power moves are beyond. We're talking inconceivable, incomparable, immeasurable—the kind of thing that makes you question everything you thought you knew."

Then Ānanda caught a whiff of something divine and was like, "What is this fragrance though? It's giving me life I didn't even know I needed."

The Buddha spilled the tea: "That's coming from these Bodhisattvas' pores, honey. When you're that enlightened, even your sweat is couture."

Sariputra jumped in: "Actually, we're all giving that same fragrance right now. You can thank Vimalakīrti for that—he got us some leftovers from that fancy universe up there, and now everyone who had a taste is serving aromatic excellence."

Ānanda, still living for the fragrance moment, asked Vimalakīrti how long this divine smell was gonna last.

"Until the food's digested," Vimalakīrti said, casual as anything. "And before you ask—it'll take seven days and seven nights. But don't worry about getting bloated or anything—this is spiritual food we're talking about. It's not gonna do you dirty like that 3am taco truck run."

But that wasn't the gag—Vimalakīrti went on to explain that this wasn't your regular degular food. This was that transformative cuisine. If you hadn't stepped into your enlightenment era yet, you wouldn't digest it until you did. If you were still caught up in your desires, you had to work through that first. It was like a spiritual Weight Watchers, but instead of counting points, you were counting enlightenment moments.

"Listen," Vimalakīrti said, "this is like that one medicinal tea that won't leave your system until it's cleared out all the toxins. Except instead of physical toxins, we're talking about the poison of your messy passions. The food stays until the spiritual work is done."

Ānanda was shook. He turned to the Buddha like, "This is beyond. This food isn't feeding bodies, it's feeding souls."

The Buddha nodded. "That's exactly the tea, Ānanda. And it's not just happening here—this kind of spiritual seasoning is going down in Buddha-fields all over the cosmos."

Then he started breaking down how different Buddha-fields work their magic. Some do it through Bodhisattvas serving looks, others through divine light shows. Some use enlightenment trees like they're spiritual Pinterest, others just flash the Buddha's perfect features. You've got your food moments, your water features, your divine architecture—basically, every Buddha-field has its own way of getting beings to wake tf up.

Some fields were teaching through words, others through straight-up silence. It was like having different professors—some lecture, some make you do the work yourself, but they're all trying to get you to graduate from ignorance university.

The Buddha explained how every field had its own vibe but was working the same job—getting beings to recognize their own divine nature. It was like different drag houses with different styles but all serving excellence in their own way.

Then Ānanda had this moment where he checked his own privilege. He was like, "Damn, maybe I shouldn't be out here calling myself the smartest in the room when these Bodhisattvas are operating on levels I can't even comprehend."

The Buddha was quick with the validation though: "Baby, when I called you the smartest, I meant among the Śrāvakas. These Bodhisattvas are playing a whole different game. Trying to measure their wisdom is like trying to empty the ocean with a teaspoon—cute effort, but not gonna happen."

Then all those Bodhisattvas who'd come from the Sarvagandhasugandhā universe were like, "We need to confess something. When we first got here, we were kind of judging your universe for being basic. But now we're feeling real embarrassed about that, because we see that the Buddhas work in mysterious ways, serving different looks for different folks."

The Buddha gave them what they needed—a teaching about the exhaustible and inexhaustible. It was this whole moment about how you can't just check out of the messy world (that's the exhaustible part) but you also can't get too caught up in it (that's the inexhaustible tea).

He broke it down like this: A good Bodhisattva, much like that friend who is ever-present at every protest, standing in solidarity while also mastering the art of self-care, navigates the world with a deft hand. They are the embodiment of engaged presence, a beacon of hope amidst the chaos, helping others while maintaining an unwavering commitment to their own spiritual journey. In the thick of it all, they serve compassion with an effortless grace, their wisdom remaining untouched by the tumult around them. They work within the fabric of society, deftly maneuvering through its complexities, yet they remain untethered by its transient nature, transcending the ordinary while grounded in the profound. They walk the line between action and reflection, embodying a duality that is as inspiring as it is necessary in these times of change and awakening.

"Look," he said, "you've got to find that sweet spot between doing the work and not getting burned out by it. It's like being at a circuit party—you want to dance all night but you also need to stay hydrated."

With a voice that resonated like the tolling of a great bell, the Buddha proceeded to unfurl a tapestry of wisdom, each thread a guideline for the harmonious balance of a Bodhisattva's path. It was as if he had plucked the very stars from the night sky to illuminate the way.

Firstly, he spoke of the boundless well of goodwill that must be tended with care, not as a finite pool to be depleted, but as a river that flows with ceaseless generosity. "Let your benevolence be like the Ganges," he advised, "ever-moving, ever-replenishing, nurturing the soil of all beings without ever running dry."

Next, he addressed the heart of compassion, likening it to the eternal flame of a lighthouse, steadfast and unwavering, yet considerate of its own fuel. "Compassion," he explained, "must be sustainable, a garden that is lovingly tended, so that its blossoms may continue to offer solace to weary travelers."

Then, with a gaze that pierced through the illusions of the material world, he spoke of aiding others without succumbing to the erosion of one's own spirit. "To uplift others is divine," he said, "but remember, the vessel that pours must not itself become empty."

With a smile that held the secrets of the universe, the Buddha wove the delicate balance between authenticity and sanctity. "Keep it real," he urged, "for honesty is the bedrock upon which true spirituality is built. Yet, in your realness, do not forget to consecrate your actions, for holiness is the light that guides the ship of your soul through treacherous waters."

As he spoke of staying grounded while reaching for the heavens, his words were like the roots of the Bodhi Tree, deep in the earth yet stretching towards the boundless sky. "Stand firm," he counseled, "with your feet planted in the rich soil of the present moment, while your aspirations soar into the celestial expanse, for in this duality lies the dance of enlightenment."

Finally, with a twinkle in his eye that suggested the cosmos itself was in on some delightful secret, the Buddha spoke of the divine plan, a blueprint for existence that was both ancient and ever-new. "Work this plan with the dedication of an artisan," he said, "and make it fashion, for the universe delights in the unique expression of your being, and your life is the canvas upon which the divine paints its masterpiece."

And with these words, the Buddha folded his hands, the embodiment of peace and purpose, leaving the assembly to ponder the profound simplicity of his teachings, each soul contemplating how to weave these threads into the fabric of their own existence.

When he finished spilling all this tea, those visiting Bodhisattvas were living. They covered the whole universe knee-deep in divine offerings—celestial flower petals, sacred incense, the works. They did their final bows, circled the Buddha three times like they were closing a spell, and then disappeared back to their fancy fragrant universe faster than you can say "enlightenment."

1 2

The Whole Truth Buffet

The Buddha was giving Vimalakirti that look. You know the one, like when your wisest friend is about to drop some truth on you.

"So," Buddha said, casual as someone asking about your lunch plans, with wisdom behind his eyes, "now that you're here looking at me, what do you see?"

This wasn't just some random question. He wasn't asking about his physical appearance or the man who'd walked away from palace life to find truth under a tree. He was asking about something deeper: what's the real nature of an awakened one?

Vimalakirti, who had that energy of someone who saw through everything, took a moment. His silence filled the room like incense smoke, curling around the edges of reality.

"Let me tell you something about seeing the Buddha," he said, settling into his seat like someone about to explain quantum physics using grocery store items. "When I truly look at the awakened one, it's like looking at... nothing. And before you think I'm throwing shade, let me break it down."

He gestured at the air around them, which started shimmering like heat waves off summer asphalt. "The Buddha isn't stuck in time like we are. He's not checking his calendar for next week or scrolling through memories of last year. He's free from all that past-present-future business."

The air in the room got thick with truth, heavy like humidity before a summer storm. "Look, when most of us see things, we get caught up in labels and categories. We see a cup and think 'cup.' We see a tree and think 'tree.' But the Buddha's different. He's like pure awareness itself – present in everything but not stuck to anything. Like your reflection in water. You can see yourself, but try to grab it and your hands come up empty."

Vimalakirti was on a roll now, his words rearranging reality like someone reorganizing a convenience store shelf to reveal the secrets of the universe. "You won't find him by looking for a physical form. He's more like the space that holds everything – the awareness that makes all experience possible."

The walls of reality were soft around the edges, like ice cream left out in the sun. "The Buddha's consciousness isn't limited like ours. He's not scrolling through life's feed looking for likes. He's not trying to level up or gain followers. He's free, totally awake, seeing everything exactly as it is."

"It's like this," Vimalakirti continued, picking up an imaginary glass, "when you're thirsty, you might dream about water. But once you're drinking, you don't need the dream anymore. The Buddha's like someone who's quenched all spiritual thirst – he doesn't need concepts or ideas about reality because he's living it directly."

Then Sariputra, who never met a deep question he didn't like, jumped in like someone trying to get the last word in a group chat: "So where were you before you came to our universe?"

The Buddha gave him that look—you know the one, like when someone asks about the recipe after they've already changed every ingredient. "Why don't you ask him yourself?"

So Sariputra turned to Vimalakirti: "Where'd you come from before showing up here?"

Vimalakirti served him this reality check with a side of wisdom: "In all your spiritual searching, have you ever seen life appear from pure nothingness? Or is it more like watching a garden - where a flower doesn't just *poof* into being, but unfolds from a seed, which came from another flower, which grew from the earth, which was nourished by rain that was once ocean? Even you, with all your wisdom, weren't created from nothing—you're a dance of your parents' love, the food you've eaten, the air you've breathed, the stories you've heard."

"No," Sariputra had to admit, looking like someone who just realized they'd been reading the story of existence backwards. "Everything flows from everything else."

"Then why are you asking about where I came from? It's like this—if someone created a perfect virtual world and someone asked where that world was before it appeared on screen, what would they say?"

The Buddha, who'd been watching this whole exchange like a master chef watching someone discover salt for the first time, finally spoke up: "He came from another universe—a pure one, where everything's already awakened. He came here to help others wake up too."

Sariputra couldn't help himself: "Wild that someone would leave paradise to come to our messy corner of existence."

But Vimalakirti wasn't having it: "Does light avoid dark rooms? That's its whole job description. Those who are awake show up where they're needed, like a friend bringing a flashlight when the power's out."

Everyone got curious about this other universe then, like when someone mentions a secret restaurant that serves happiness on a plate. The Buddha, reading the room like a book written in neon, turned to Vimalakirti: "Show them what you're working with."

What happened next was pure cosmic magic. Vimalakirti, still chilling like it was Sunday afternoon, reached out with his mind and pulled an entire universe into view. Imagine someone picking up a snow globe, but the snow globe contains galaxies, mountains, rivers, and beings of light.

When the two universes merged, they didn't get cramped or crowded. They just... coexisted, like when you figure out how to organize your closet and suddenly everything fits.

The Buddha gave everyone the grand tour: "This is what it looks like when everything and everyone is awake."

After the cosmic show-and-tell, Vimalakirti put everything back in its place, neat as someone returning a borrowed book. As the universes separated, both sides got one last look at each other, like old friends saying goodbye after the best conversation of their lives.

The whole experience had everyone catching feelings for awakening like it was the latest viral sensation. Sariputra was fully convinced: "Everyone should get to experience this level of reality. This isn't just truth—this is the whole truth buffet."

Analysis: Vimalakirti For A Modern World

The stories of Vimalakirti's teaching moments flow through Buddhist history like honey, sweet with wisdom and sticky with truth. Each one shows us something profound about how awakening works, especially when you're living right in the middle of the world instead of hiding away in a cave.

These ancient stories light up our modern lives in ways that feel almost prophetic. For those of us living queer lives today, Vimalakirti's teachings hit different. We know something about playing roles while staying true to our deepest nature. We understand what it means to transform the very things society calls problems into sources of power and beauty.

When Vimalakirti teaches from his sickbed about transforming suffering, every queer person who's had to navigate a world that sometimes treats their very existence as an illness feels that truth in their bones. But like Vimalakirti, we know that our greatest challenges can become our greatest teachings. Every time we turn pain into pride, every time we transform rejection into community, every time we make art from adversity—we're walking his path.

His empty room becomes a mirror for how we've had to let go of so many society's fixed ideas about gender, sexuality, and identity. When you've had to empty yourself of what everyone told you you're supposed to be, just to find out who you really are—that's Vimalakirti's teaching living through you. And when you learn to be comfortable in that emptiness, to find freedom in that space where rigid definitions fall away? Baby, that's enlightenment calling.

Think about those celestial flowers that stuck to people who couldn't let go of their ideas about purity and impurity. How many of us have had to deal with other people's hang-ups about what's "natural" or "proper" or "normal"? Vimalakirti's teaching shows us that the real problem isn't who we are, it's the rigid thinking that can't handle our truth. The flowers aren't the issue; the attachment to fixed categories is.

And then there's that profound silence when asked about non-duality. For queer folks who've always known that binaries don't tell the whole story—whether it's gender, sexuality, or any other either/or that society tries to force on us—that silence speaks volumes. Sometimes the truest answer to "what are you?" is simply to exist, beautifully and unapologetically, beyond the categories.

The beauty of Vimalakirti's teachings is that they're not just nice stories, they're invitations to practice. And this practice isn't about sitting on a cushion pretending the world doesn't exist. It's about transforming every moment, every challenge, every bit of shade thrown your way into an opportunity for awakening.

Start with your own "illness," whatever that means for you. Maybe it's actual physical challenges. Maybe it's society's reaction to your queerness. Maybe it's just the basic suffering of being alive in samsara. Whatever it is, Vimalakirti shows us how to work with it. Instead of fighting it or trying to transcend it, make it your teaching seat. Let it be the place from which you understand and connect with others who are also suffering. Every time someone comes to you with their pain, let your own challenges be the source of genuine compassion.

When you're moving through different spaces – work, family, queer community, spiritual circles—remember Vimalakirti's skillful performances. Each role you play can be both authentic and enlightening. That code-switching you do? That's not fake, it's skillful means. You're learning to speak each community's language while staying true to your deepest nature. The key is to remember that you're not stuck in any of these role, you're consciously choosing them as ways to connect and serve.

And about that divine shade? Vimalakirti shows us how to transform even our reads into wisdom teachings. When you need to check someone, do it with compassion so fierce it burns away delusion. Let your critiques come from love, not spite. Make your callouts wake people up, not shut them down.

Then there's that powerful teaching on emptiness—the understanding that nothing has a fixed, inherent nature. For queer folks, this isn't just philosophy. We live this truth every time we refuse to be limited by society's labels, every time we create ourselves anew, every time we show that gender, sexuality, and identity are more fluid and spacious than anyone imagined. Our very lives become teachings about freedom from fixed concepts.

BRINGING VIMALAKIRTI INTO YOUR PRACTICE

When it comes to actual practice, Vimalakirti's approach is all about transmutation—turning everything into the path. Here's how we can work with this in our own lives:

Start your day by touching your own suffering—whatever it is—with tenderness. Sit with it like Vimalakirti on his couch. Don't try to fix it or transcend it. Just feel it fully and let it connect you to everyone else who's experiencing similar pain. This isn't about wallowing; it's about using your challenges as a bridge to universal compassion.

Throughout your day, practice what we might call "sacred shade awareness." When you feel judgment arising—whether towards yourself or others—pause. Notice how that judgment feels in your body. Then, like Vimalakirti, ask yourself: Could this moment of critique become a teaching? Could this sharp observation be turned into medicine? Remember how he never tore people down, he used his reads to wake them up to greater possibilities.

In meditation, play with Vimalakirti's empty room. Start by noticing all the mental furniture you're constantly rearranging—your ideas about who you are, what you should be, how spirituality should look. Then, piece by piece, let it all go. Not forever, just for this moment. Sit in the spaciousness that remains. Notice how much more room there is to breathe when you're not trying to maintain an image of yourself.

When you're out in the world playing different roles, bring awareness to each performance. Notice how you shift your energy in different spaces. Instead of judging this as fake or real, see it as skillful means. Like Vimalakirti in the palace, the marketplace, the brothels, and the temples—you're adapting your expression to serve each situation while remaining rooted in your true nature.

And perhaps most importantly, practice what we might call "fierce compassion." When you see someone trapped in self-judgment or internalized oppression, let your heart break open. Then let that broken-openness fuel your determination to help them wake up to their inherent dignity. Sometimes this might look like gentleness. Sometimes it might look like a reality check served with style. Trust your wisdom to know which is needed.

Remember, Vimalakirti's ultimate teaching was silence. So end each practice session by dropping all techniques, all striving, all ideas about spirituality. Just rest in the simple awareness that's already present, already free, already complete. Let that silence teach you what words never can.

In the end, Vimalakirti's story isn't just about an iconic figure from Buddhist literature. It's about all of us trying to find liberation in the middle of the mess. It's about transforming everything—our struggles, our fabulousness, our shade, our silence—into the path of awakening.

Maybe you won't empty out your apartment and teach dharma from a fabulous couch. Maybe you won't summon goddesses to rain flowers on unsuspecting spiritual materialists. But you can let your life be a teaching. You can let your authenticity challenge others' fixed ideas. You can transform suffering into compassion. You can make art from adversity. You can serve truth with style.

The real miracle in Vimalakirti's story isn't the magical feasts or the cosmic displays. It's the simple fact that liberation doesn't require us to be anyone other than who we are. We don't have to choose between being queer and being spiritual. We don't have to pick between engagement and enlightenment. Every aspect of our lives—yes, every single one—can be part of the path.

May this story remind you that the very things society might call your problems can become your sources of wisdom. May it show you that you can be both fierce and compassionate, both engaged and free.

Your authentic self, in all its complexity and beauty, is not an obstacle to awakening. It is the very path itself.

Let me spill some tea about our fierce author, David Franklin Sparks! This multifaceted artist isn't just serving one type of realness - he's a Buddhist practitioner, writer, musician, and drag performer who knows how to werk it in multiple venues, honey. As the musical artist dFRAE and the drag persona Fancy Sparkles, David brings creativity and authenticity to everything he touches.

After years of studying and practicing Buddhism while navigating queer life, David saw the need for a spiritual guide that spoke our language. That's what led him to write the Queering the Path to Enlightenment book series, and start the Queer Dharma Library, bringing together his love for Buddhism and his commitment to the LGBTQ+ community.

When he's not busy making the Dharma fabulous or producing indie pop bops, David's probably somewhere Out there being his full-grown self!

QUEERING THE PATH TO ENLIGHTENMENT
- Book 1: From Drama to Dharma
- Book 2: Breaking Free
- Book 3: Compassion That Walk!

QUEER DHARMA LIBRARY
- Queering Shantideva's the Way of the Bodhisattva
- The Reading of Vimalakirti